A HACKER

MANIFESTO

A HACKER MANIFESTO

McKenzie Wark

HARVARD UNIVERSITY PRESS

Cambridge, Massachusetts, and London, England

2004

Thanks to: AG, AR, BH, BL, CD, CF, the late CH, CL, CS, DB, DG, DS, FB, FS, GG, GL, HJ, IV, JB, JD, JF, JR, KH, KS, LW, MD, ME, MH, MI, MT, MV, NR, OS, PM, RD, RG, RN, RS, SB, SD, SH, SK, SL, SS, TB, TC, TW.

Earlier versions of *A Hacker Manifesto* appeared in *Critical Secret, Feelergauge, Fibreculture Reader, Sarai Reader* and *Subsol*.

Printed in the United States of America

Library of Congress Cataloging-in-Publication Data
Wark, McKenzie, 1961–
    A hacker manifesto / McKenzie Wark.
        p. cm.
    ISBN 0-674-01543-6 (hc : alk. paper)
    1. Digital divide. 2. Computer hackers. 3. Social conflict.
  4. Intellectual property. 5. Information technology—Social aspects.
  6. Computers and civilization. I. Title.
HC79.I55W37 2004
303.48'33—dc22   2004047488

In memoriam:

Kathy

King of the Pirates

Acker

This land is your land, this land is my land
—WOODY GUTHRIE

This land is your land, this land is my land
—GANG OF FOUR

This land is your land, this land is my land
—LUTHER BLISSETT

. . . it sort of springs organically from the earth.
And it has the characteristics of communism, that
people love so very much about it. That is, it's free.
—STEVE BALLMER, CEO, Microsoft

A HACKER

MANIFESTO

A B S T R A C T I O N

A double spooks the world, the double of abstraction. The fortunes of states and armies, companies and communities depend on it. All contending classes, be they ruling or ruled, revere it—yet fear it. Ours is a world that ventures blindly into the new with its fingers crossed. [001]

All classes fear this relentless abstraction of the world, on which their fortunes yet depend. All classes but one: the hacker class. We are the hackers of abstraction. We produce new concepts, new perceptions, new sensations, hacked out of raw data. Whatever code we hack, be it programming language, poetic language, math or music, curves or colorings, we are the abstracters of new worlds. Whether we come to represent ourselves as researchers or authors, artists or biologists, chemists or musicians, philosophers or programmers, each of these subjectivities is but a fragment of a class still becoming, bit by bit, aware of itself as such. [002]

And yet we don't quite know who we are. That is why this book seeks to make manifest our origins, our purpose and our interests. A hacker manifesto: Not the only manifesto, as it is in the nature of the hacker to differ from others, to differ even from oneself, over time. To hack is to differ. A [003] hacker manifesto cannot claim to represent what refuses representation.

[004] Hackers create the possibility of new things entering the world. Not always great things, or even good things, but new things. In art, in science, in philosophy and culture, in any production of knowledge where data can be gathered, where information can be extracted from it, and where in that information new possibilities for the world produced, there are hackers hacking the new out of the old. While we create these new worlds, we do not possess them. That which we create is mortgaged to others, and to the interests of others, to states and corporations who monopolize the means for making worlds we alone discover. We do not own what we produce—it owns us.

[005] Hackers use their knowledge and their wits to maintain their autonomy. Some take the money and run. (We must live with our compromises.) Some refuse to compromise. (We live as best we can.) All too often those of us who take one of these paths resent those who take the other. One lot resents the prosperity it lacks, the other resents the liberty it lacks to hack away at the world freely. What eludes the hacker class is a more abstract expression of our interests as a class, and of how this interest may meet those of others in the world.

[006] Hackers are not joiners. We're not often willing to submerge our singularity. What the times call for is a collective hack that realizes a class interest based on an alignment of differences rather than a coercive unity. Hackers are a class,

but an abstract class. A class that makes abstractions, and a class made abstract. To abstract hackers as a class is to abstract the very concept of class itself. The slogan of the hacker class is not the workers of the world united, but the workings of the world untied.

Everywhere abstraction reigns, abstraction made concrete. [007] Everywhere abstraction's straight lines and pure curves order matters along complex but efficient vectors. But where education teaches what one may produce with an abstraction, the knowledge most useful for the hacker class is of how abstractions are themselves produced. Deleuze: "Abstractions explain nothing, they themselves have to be explained."*

Abstraction may be discovered or produced, may be mate- [008] rial or immaterial, but abstraction is what every hack produces and affirms. To abstract is to construct a plane upon which otherwise different and unrelated matters may be brought into many possible relations. To abstract is to express the virtuality of nature, to make known some instance of its possibilities, to actualize a relation out of infinite relationality, to manifest the manifold.

History is the production of abstraction and the abstrac- [009] tion of production. What makes life differ in one age after the next is the application of new modes of abstraction to the task of wresting freedom from necessity. History is the virtual made actual, one hack after another. History is the cumulative qualitative differentiation of nature as it is hacked.

[010] Out of the abstraction of nature comes its productivity, and the production of a surplus over and above the necessities of survival. Out of this expanding surplus over necessity comes an expanding capacity to hack, again and again, producing further abstractions, further productivity, further release from necessity—at least in potential. But the hacking of nature, the production of surplus, does not make us free. Again and again, a ruling class arises that controls the surplus over bare necessity and enforces new necessities on those peoples who produce this very means of escaping necessity.

[011] What makes our times different is the appearance on the horizon of possibility of a new world, long imagined—a world free from necessity. The production of abstraction has reached the threshold where it can break the shackles holding hacking fast to outdated and regressive class interests, once and for all. Debord: "The world already possesses the dream of a time whose consciousness it must now possess in order to actually live it."*

[012] Invention is the mother of necessity. While all states depend on abstraction for the production of their wealth and power, the ruling class of any given state has an uneasy relationship to the production of abstraction in new forms. The ruling class seeks always to control innovation and turn it to its own ends, depriving the hacker of control of her or his creation, and thereby denying the world as a whole the right to manage its own development.

[013] The production of new abstraction always takes place among those set apart by the act of hacking. We others who

have hacked new worlds out of old, in the process become not merely strangers apart but a class apart. While we recognize our distinctive existence as a group, as programmers or artists or writers or scientists or musicians, we rarely see these ways of representing ourselves as mere fragments of a class experience. Geeks and freaks become what they are negatively, through exclusion by others. Together we form a class, a class as yet to hack itself into existence as itself—and for itself.

 It is through the abstract that the virtual is identified, produced and released. The virtual is not just the potential latent in matter, it is the potential of potential. To hack is to produce or apply the abstract to information and express the possibility of new worlds, beyond necessity. [014]

All abstractions are abstractions of nature. Abstractions release the potential of the material world. And yet abstraction relies on the material world's most curious quality—information. Information can exist independently of a given material form, but cannot exist without any material form. It is at once material and immaterial. The hack depends on the material qualities of nature, and yet discovers something independent of a given material form. It is at once material and immaterial. It discovers the immaterial virtuality of the material, its qualities of information. [015]

Abstraction is always an abstraction of nature, a process that creates nature's double, a second nature, a space of human existence in which collective life dwells among its own products and comes to take the environment it produces to be natural. [016]

[017] Land is the detachment of a resource from nature, an aspect of the productive potential of nature rendered abstract, in the form of property. Capital is the detachment of a resource from land, an aspect of the productive potential of land rendered abstract in the form of property. Information is the detachment of a resource from capital already detached from land. It is the double of a double. It is a further process of abstraction beyond capital, but one that yet again produces its separate existence in the form of property.

[018] Just as the development of land as a productive resource creates the historical advances for its abstraction in the form of capital, so too does the development of capital provide the historical advances for the further abstraction of information, in the form of "intellectual property." In traditional societies, land, capital and information were bound to particular social or regional powers by customary or hereditary ties. What abstraction hacks out of the old feudal carcass is a liberation of these resources based on a more abstract form of property, a universal right to private property. This universal abstract form encompasses first land, then capital, now information.

[019] When the abstraction of property unleashes productive resources, it produces at the same time a class division. Private property establishes a pastoralist class that owns the land, and a farmer class dispossessed of it. Out of the people the abstraction of private property expells from its traditional communal right to land, it creates a dispossessed class who become the working class, as they are set to work by a rising class of owners of the material means of manufacturing, the

capitalist class. This working class becomes the first class to seriously entertain the notion of overthrowing class rule. It fails in this historic task to the extent that the property form is not yet abstract enough to release the virtuality of class-lessness that is latent in the productive energies of abstraction itself.

It is always the hack that creates a new abstraction. With the emergence of a hacker class, the rate at which new abstractions are produced accelerates. The recognition of intellectual property as a form of property—itself an abstraction, a legal hack—creates a class of intellectual property creators. But this class still labors for the benefit of another class, to whose interests its own interests are subordinated. As the abstraction of private property is extended to information, it produces the hacker class as a class, as a class able to make of its innovations in abstraction a form of property. Unlike farmers and workers, hackers have not—yet—been dispossessed of their property rights entirely, but still must sell their capacity for abstraction to a class that owns the means of production, the vectoralist class—the emergent ruling class of our time. [020]

The vectoralist class wages an intensive struggle to dispossess hackers of their intellectual property. Patents and copyrights all end up in the hands, not of their creators, but of a vectoralist class that owns the means of realizing the value of these abstractions. The vectoralist class struggles to monopolize abstraction. For the vectoral class, "politics is about absolute control over intellectual property by means of war-like strategies of communication, control, and command."* [021]

Hackers find themselves dispossessed both individually, and as a class.

[022] As the vectoralist class consolidates its monopoly on the means of realizing the value of intellectual property, it confronts the hacker class more and more as a class antagonist. Hackers come to struggle against the usurious charges the vectoralists extort for access to the information that hackers collectively produce, but that vectoralists come to own. Hackers come to struggle against the particular forms in which abstraction is commodified and turned into the private property of the vectoralist class. Hackers come as a class to recognize their class interest is best expressed through the struggle to free the production of abstraction, not just from the particular fetters of this or that form of property, but to abstract the form of property itself.

[023] The time is past due when hackers must come together with workers and farmers—with all of the producers of the world—to liberate productive and inventive resources from the myth of scarcity. The time is past due for new forms of association to be created that can steer the world away from its destruction through commodified exploitation. The greatest hacks of our time may turn out to be forms of organizing free collective expression, so that from this time on, abstraction serves the people, rather than the people serving the ruling class.

CLASS

A class arises—the working class—able to question the [024] necessity of private property. A party arises, within the worker's movement, claiming to answer to working class desires—the communists. As Marx writes, "in all these movements they bring to the front, as the leading question in each, the property question, no matter what its degree of development at the time." This was the answer communists proposed to the property question: "centralize all instruments of production in the hands of the state."* Making property a state monopoly only produced a new ruling class, and a new and more brutal class struggle. But is that our final answer? Perhaps the course of the class struggle is not yet over. Perhaps there is another class that can open the property question in a new way—and in keeping the question open end once and for all the monopoly of the ruling classes on the ends of history.

There is a class dynamic driving each stage of the develop- [025] ment of this vectoral world in which we now find ourselves. The vectoral class is driving this world to the brink of disaster, but it also opens up the world to the resources for overcoming its own destructive tendencies. In the three successive phases of commodification, quite different ruling classes arise, usurping different forms of private property. Each ruling class in turn drives the world towards ever more abstract ends.

[026] First arises a pastoralist class. They disperse the great mass of peasants who traditionally worked the land under the thumb of feudal lords. The pastoralists supplant the feudal lords, releasing the productivity of nature that they claim as their private property. It is this privatization of property—a legal hack—that creates the conditions for every other hack by which the land is made to yield a surplus. A vectoral world rises on the shoulders of the agricultural hack.

[027] As new forms of abstraction make it possible to produce a surplus from the land with fewer and fewer farmers, pastoralists turn them off their land, depriving them of their livelihood. Dispossessed farmers seek work and a new home in cities. Here capital puts them to work in its factories. Farmers become workers. Capital as property gives rise to a class of capitalists who own the means of production, and a class of workers, dispossessed of it—and by it. Whether as workers or farmers, the direct producers find themselves dispossessed not only of their land, but of the greater part of the surplus they produce, which accumulates to the pastoralists in the form of rent as the return on land, and to capitalists in the form of profit as the return on capital.

[028] Dispossessed farmers become workers, only to be dispossessed again. Having lost their agriculture, they lose in turn their human culture. Capital produces in its factories not just the necessities of existence, but a way of life it expects

its workers to consume. Commodified life dispossess the worker of the information traditionally passed on outside the realm of private property as culture, as the gift of one generation to the next, and replaces it with information in commodified form.

Information, like land or capital, becomes a form of prop- [029] erty monopolized by a class, a class of vectoralists, so named because they control the vectors along which information is abstracted, just as capitalists control the material means with which goods are produced, and pastoralists the land with which food is produced. This information, once the collective property of the productive classes—the working and farming classes considered together—becomes the property of yet another appropriating class.

As peasants become farmers through the appropriation of [030] their land, they still retain some autonomy over the disposition of their working time. Workers, even though they do not own capital, and must work according to the clock and its merciless time, could at least struggle to reduce the working day and release free time from labor. Information circulated within working class culture as a public property belonging to all. But when information in turn becomes a form of private property, workers are dispossessed of it, and must buy their own culture back from its owners, the vectoralist class. The farmer becomes a worker, and the worker, a slave. The whole world becomes subject to the extraction of a surplus from the producing classes that is controlled by the ruling classes, who use it merely to reproduce and expand this matrix of exploitation. Time itself becomes a commodified experience.

[031] The producing classes—farmers, workers, hackers—struggle against the expropriating classes—pastoralists, capitalists, vectoralists—but these successive ruling classes struggle also amongst themselves. Capitalists try to break the pastoral monopoly on land and subordinate the produce of the land to industrial production. Vectoralists try to break capital's monopoly on the production process, and subordinate the production of goods to the circulation of information: "The privileged realm of electronic space controls the physical logistics of manufacture, since the release of raw materials and manufactured goods requires electronic consent and direction."*

[032] That the vectoralist class has replaced capital as the dominant exploiting class can be seen in the form that the leading corporations take. These firms divest themselves of their productive capacity, as this is no longer a source of power. They rely on a competing mass of capitalist contractors for the manufacture of their products. Their power lies in monopolizing intellectual property—patents, copyrights and trademarks—and the means of reproducing their value—the vectors of communication. The privatization of information becomes the dominant, rather than a subsidiary, aspect of commodified life. "There is a certain logic to this progression: first, a select group of manufacturers transcend their connection to earthbound products, then, with marketing elevated as the pinnacle of their business, they attempt to alter marketing's social status as a commercial interruption and replace it with seamless integration."* With the rise of the vectoral class, the vectoral world is complete.

As private property advances from land to capital to infor- [033] mation, property itself becomes more abstract. Capital as property frees land from its spatial fixity. Information as property frees capital from its fixity in a particular object. This abstraction of property makes property itself something amenable to accelerated innovation—and conflict. Class conflict fragments, but creeps into any and every relation that becomes a relation of property. The property question, the basis of class, becomes the question asked everywhere, of everything. If "class" appears absent to the apologists of our time, it is not because it has become just another in a series of antagonisms and articulations, but on the contrary because it has become the structuring principle of the vectoral plane which organizes the play of identities as differences.

The hacker class, producer of new abstractions, becomes [034] more important to each successive ruling class, as each depends more and more on information as a resource. Land cannot be reproduced at will. Good land lends itself to scarcity, and the abstraction of private property is almost enough on its own to protect the rents of the pastoral class. Capital's profits rest on mechanically reproducible means of production, its factories and inventories. The capitalist firm sometimes needs the hacker to refine and advance the tools and techniques of productions to stay abreast of the competition. Information is the most easily reproducible object ever captured in the abstraction of property. Nothing protects the vectoralist business from its competitors other than its capacity to qualitatively transform the information it possesses and extract new value from it. The services of the hacker class become indispensable to an economy that is it-self more and more dispensable—an economy of property and scarcity.

[035]   As the means of production become more abstract, so too does the property form. Property has to expand to contain more and more complex forms of difference, and reduce it to equivalence. To render land equivalent, it is enough to draw up its boundaries, and create a means of assigning it as an object to a subject. Complexities will arise, naturally, from this unnatural imposition on the surface of the world, although the principle is a simple abstraction. But for some-thing to be represented as intellectual property, it is not enough for it to be in a different location. It must be qualita-tively different. That difference, which makes a copyright or a patent possible, is the work of the hacker class. The hacker class makes what Bateson calls "the difference that makes the difference."* The difference that drives the abstraction of the world, but which also drives the accumulation of class power in the hands of the vectoral class.

[036]   The hacker class arises out of the transformation of infor-mation into property, in the form of intellectual property. This legal hack makes of the hack a property producing pro-cess, and thus a class producing process. The hack produces the class force capable of asking—and answering—the prop-erty question, the hacker class. The hacker class is the class with the capacity to create not only new kinds of object and subject in the world, not only new kinds of property form in which they may be represented, but new kinds of relation,

with unforseen properties, which question the property form itself. The hacker class realizes itself as a class when it hacks the abstraction of property and overcomes the limitations of existing forms of property.

The hacker class may be flattered by the attention lavished [037] upon it by capitalists compared to pastoralists, and vectoralists compared to capitalists. Hackers tend to ally at each turn with the more abstract form of property and commodity relation. But hackers soon feel the restrictive grip of each ruling class, as it secures its dominance over its predecessor and rival, and can renege on the dispensations it extended to hackers as a class. The vectoralist class, in particular, will go out of its way to court and coopt the productivity of hackers, but only because of its attenuated dependence on new abstraction as the engine of competition among vectoral interests. When the vectoralists act in concert as a class it is to subject hacking to the prerogatives of its class power.

The vectoral world is dynamic. It puts new abstractions to [038] work, producing new freedoms from necessity. The direction this struggle takes is not given in the course of things, but is determined by the struggle between classes. All classes enter into relations of conflict, collusion and compromise. Their relations are not necessarily dialectical. Classes may form alliances of mutual interest against other classes, or may arrive at a "historic compromise," for a time. Yet despite pauses and setbacks, the class struggle drives history into abstraction and abstraction into history.

[039] Sometimes capital forms an alliance with the pastoralists, and the two classes effectively merge under the leadership of the capitalist interest. Sometimes capital forms an alliance with workers against the pastoralist class, an alliance quickly broken once the dissolution of the pastoralist class is achieved. These struggles leave their traces in the historical form of the state, which maintains the domination of the ruling class interest and at the same time adjudicates among the representatives of competing classes.

[040] History is full of surprises. Sometimes—for a change—the workers form an alliance with the farmers that socializes private property and puts it in the hands of the state, while liquidating the pastoralist and capitalist classes. In this case, the state then becomes a collective pastoralist and capitalist class, and wields class power over a commodity economy organized on a bureaucratic rather than competitive basis.

[041] The vectoralist class emerges out of competitive, rather than bureaucratic states. Competitive conditions drive the search for productive abstraction more effectively. The development of abstract forms of intellectual property creates the relative autonomy in which the hacker class can produce abstractions, although this productivity is constrained within the commodity form.

[042] One thing unites pastoralists, capitalists and vectoralists— the sanctity of the property form on which class power depends. Each depends on forms of abstraction that they may buy and own but do not produce. Each comes to depend on

the hacker class, which finds new ways of making nature productive, which discovers new patterns in the data thrown off by nature and second nature, which produces new abstractions through which nature may be made to yield more of a second nature—perhaps even a third nature.

The hacker class, being numerically small and not owning the means of production, finds itself caught between a politics of the masses from below and a politics of the rulers from above. It must bargain as best it can, or do what it does best—hack out a new politics, beyond this opposition. In the long run, the interests of the hacker class are in accord with those who would benefit most from the advance of abstraction, namely those productive classes dispossessed of the means of production—farmers and workers. In the effort to realize this possibility the hacker class hacks politics itself, creating a new polity, turning mass politics into a politics of multiplicity, in which all the productive classes can express their virtuality. [043]

The hacker interest cannot easily form alliances with forms of mass politics that subordinate minority differences to unity in action. Mass politics always run the danger of suppressing the creative, abstracting force of the interaction of differences. The hacker interest is not in mass representation, but in a more abstract politics that expresses the productivity of differences. Hackers, who produce many classes of knowledge out of many classes of experience, have the potential also to produce a new knowledge of class formation and action when working together with the collective experience of all the productive classes. [044]

[045] A class is not the same as its representation. In politics one must beware of representations held out to be classes, which represent only a fraction of a class and do not express its multiple interests. Classes do not have vanguards that may speak for them. Classes express themselves equally in all of their multiple interests and actions. The hacker class is not what it is; the hacker class is what it is not—but can become.

[046] Through the development of abstraction, freedom may yet be wrested from necessity. The vectoralist class, like its predecessors, seeks to shackle abstraction to the production of scarcity and margin, not abundance and liberty. The formation of the hacker class as a class comes at just this moment when freedom from necessity and from class domination appears on the horizon as a possibility. Negri: "What is this world of political, ideological and productive crisis, this world of sublimation and uncontrollable circulation? What is it, then, if not an epoch-making leap beyond everything humanity has hitherto experienced? . . . It constitutes simultaneously the ruin and the new potential of all meaning."* All that it takes is the hacking of the hacker class as a class, a class capable of hacking property itself, which is the fetter upon all productive means and on the productivity of meaning.

[047] The struggle among classes has hitherto determined the disposition of the surplus, the regime of scarcity and the form in which production grows. But now the stakes are far higher. Survival and liberty are both on the horizon at once. The ruling classes turn not just the producing classes into an

instrumental resource, but nature itself, to the point where class exploitation and the exploitation of nature become the same unsustainable objectification. The potential of a class-divided world to produce its own overcoming comes not a moment too soon.

EDUCATION

Education is slavery. Education enchains the mind and makes it a resource for class power. The nature of the enslavement will reflect the current state of the class struggle for knowledge, within the apparatus of education. [048]

The pastoralist class resists education, other than as indoctrination in obedience. Its interest in education stops short at the pastors who police the sheeplike morals it would instil in the human flock that tends its grain—and sheep. [049]

When capital requires "hands" to do its dirty work, education merely trains useful hands to tend machines, and docile bodies meant to accept as natural the social order in which they find themselves. When capital requires brains, both to run its increasingly complex operations and to apply themselves to the work of consuming its products, more time spent in the prison house of education is required for admission to the ranks of the paid working class. When capital discovers that many tasks can be performed by casual employees with little training, education splits into a minimal system meant to teach servility to the poorest workers and a competitive system offering the brighter workers a way up the slippery slope to security and consumption. When the [050] ruling class preaches the necessity of an education it invariably means an education in necessity.

[051] The so-called "middle class" achieve their privileged access to consumption and security through education, in which they are obliged to invest a substantial part of their income, acquiring as their property a degree which represents the sorry fact that "the candidate can tolerate boredom and knows how to follow rules."* But most remain workers, even though they grep information rather than pick cotton or bend metal. They work in factories, but are trained to think of them as offices. They take home wages, but are trained to think of it as a salary. They wear a uniform, but are trained to think of it as a suit. The only difference is that education has taught them to give different names to the instruments of exploitation, and to despise those of their own class who name them differently.

[052] Education is organized as a prestige market, in which a few scarce qualifications provide entree to the highest paid work, and everything else arranges itself in a pyramid of prestige and price below. Scarcity infects the subject with desire for education as a thing that confers a magic ability to gain a "salary" with which to acquire still more things. Through the instrument of scarcity and the hierarchical rationing of education, workers are persuaded to see education much as the ruling class would have them see it—as a privilege.

[053] Workers have a genuine interest in education that secures employment. They desire an education that contains at least

some knowledge, but often conceived of in terms of opportunity for work. Capitalists can also be heard demanding education for work. But where workers have an interest in education that gives them some capacity to move between jobs and industries, thus preserving some autonomy, capitalists demand a paring down of education to its most functional vocational elements, to the bare necessity compatible with a particular function.

The information proletariat—infoproles—stand outside [054] this demand for education as unpaid slavery that anticipates the wage slave's life. They embody a residual, antagonistic class awareness, and resist the slavery of education. They know only too well that capital has little use for them other than as the lowest paid wage slaves. They know only too well that scholars and the media treat them like objects for their idle curiosity. The infoproles resent education and live by the knowledge of the streets. They are soon known to the police.

The hacker class has an ambivalent relation to education. [055] Hackers desire knowledge, not education. The hacker comes into being through the pure liberty of knowledge in and of itself. This puts the hacker into an antagonistic relationship to the struggle on the part of the capitalist class to make education an induction into wage slavery.

Hackers may lack an understanding of the different rela- [056] tionship workers have to education, and may fall for the elitist and hierarchical culture of education, which merely reinforces its scarcity and its economic value. The hacker may be duped by the blandishments of prestige and put virtuality in the service of conformity, professional elitism in place of collective experience, and depart from the emergent culture of the hacker class. This happens when hackers make a fetish of what their education represents, rather than expressing themselves through knowledge.

[057] Education is not knowledge. Nor is it the necessary means to acquire knowledge. Knowledge may arise just as readily from everyday life. Education is the organization of knowledge within the constraints of scarcity, under the sign of property. Education turns the subjects who enter into its portals into objects of class power, functional elements who have internalized its discipline. Education turns those who resist its objectification into known and monitored objects of other regimes of objectification—the police and the soft cops of the disciplinary state. Education produces the subjectivity that meshes with the objectivity of commodified production. One may acquire an education, as if it was a thing, but one becomes knowledgeable through a process of transformation. Knowledge, as such, is only ever partially captured by education. Knowledge as a practice always eludes and exceeds it. "There is no property in thought, no proper identity, no subjective ownership."*

[058] The hack expresses knowledge in its virtuality, by producing new abstractions that do not necessarily fit the disciplinary regime that is managing and commodifying education. Knowledge at its most abstract and productive may be rare, but this rarity has nothing to do with the scarcity imposed upon it by the commodification and hierarchy of education.

The rarity of knowledge expresses the elusive multiplicity of nature itself, which refuses to be disciplined. Nature unfolds in its own time.

In their struggle for the heart and soul of the learning [059] apparatus, hackers need allies. By embracing the class demands of the workers for knowledge that equips them with the cunning and skill to work in this world, hackers can break the link between the demands of the capitalist class for the shaping of tools for its own use, and that of the workers for practical knowledge useful to their lives. This can be combined with a knowledge based in the self-understanding of the worker as a member of a class with class interests.

The cultures of the working class, even in their commodi- [060] fied form, still contain a class sensibility useful as the basis for a collective self-knowledge. The hacker working within education has the potential to gather and propagate this experience by abstracting it as knowledge. The virtuality of everyday life is the joy of the producing classes. The virtuality of the experience of knowledge is the joy that the hacker expresses through the hack. The hacker class is only enriched by the discovery of the knowledge latent in the experience of everyday working life, which can be abstracted from its commodifed form and expressed in its virtuality.

Understanding and embracing the class culture and inter- [061] ests of the working class can advance the hacker interest in many ways. It provides a numerically strong body of allies for a much more minoritarian interest in knowledge. It provides a meeting point for potential class allies. It opens the possibility of discovering the tactics of everyday hacking of the worker and farmer classes.

[062] Both workers and hackers have an interest in schooling in which resources are allocated on the socialized—and socializing—basis Marx identified: "To each according to their needs, from each according to their abilities."* No matter how divergent in their understanding of the purpose of knowledge, workers and hackers have in common an interest in resisting educational "content" that merely trains slaves for commodity production, but also in resisting the inroads the vectoralist class wishes to make into education as an "industry."

[063] Within the institutions of education, some struggle as workers against the exploitation of their labor. Others struggle to democratize the institution's governance. Others struggle to make it answerable to the needs of the productive classes. Others struggle for the autonomy of knowledge. All of these sometimes competing and conflicting demands are elements of the same struggle for knowledge that is free production in itself and yet is not just free production for itself, but rather for the productive classes.

[064] Forewarned is forearmed. In the underdeveloped world, in the south and the east, the pastoral class still turns peasants into farmers, expropriating their traditional rights and claiming land as property. Peasants still struggle to subsist in their new-found freedom from the means of survival. Capital still turns peasants into workers and exploits them to the maximum biologically possible. They produce the material

goods that the vectoral class in the overdeveloped world stamps with its logos, according to designs it protects with its patents and trademarks. All of which calls for a new pedagogy of the oppressed, and one not just aimed at making the subaltern feel better about themselves as subjects in an emerging vectoral world of multicultural spectacle, but which provides the tools for struggling against this ongoing objectification of the world's producing classes.

The ruling classes desire an educational apparatus in which [065] a prestige education can be purchased for even the most stupid heirs to the private fortune. While this may seem attractive to the better paid workers as securing a future for their children regardless of talent, in the end even they may not be able to afford the benefits of this injustice. The interests of the producing classes as a whole are in a democratic knowledge based on free access to information, and the allocation of resources based on talent rather than wealth.

Where the capitalist class sees education as a means to an [066] end, the vectoralist class sees it as an end in itself. It sees opportunities to make education a profitable industry in its own right, based on the securing of intellectual property as a form of private property. It seeks to privatize knowledge as a resource, just as it privatizes science and culture, in order to guarantee their scarcity and their value. To the vectoralists, education is just more "content" for commodification as "communication."

The vectoralist class seeks the commodification of educa- [067] tion on a global scale. The best and brightest are drawn from around the world to its factories of prestige higher learning in the overdeveloped world. The underdeveloped world rightly complains of a "brain drain," a siphoning of its intellectual resources. The general intellect is gathered and made over into the image of commodification. Those offered the liberty of the pursuit of knowledge in itself still serve the commodification of education, in that they become an advertisement for the institution that offers this freedom in exchange for the enhancement of its prestige and global marketing power.

[068] Many of the conflicts within higher education are distractions from the class politics of knowledge. Education "disciplines" knowledge, segregating it into homogenous "fields," presided over by suitably "qualified" guardians charged with policing its representations. The production of abstraction both within these fields and across their borders is managed in the interests of preserving hierarchy and prestige. Desires that might give rise to a robust testing and challenging of new abstractions is channelled into the hankering for recognition. The hacker comes to identify with his or her own commodification. Recognition becomes formal rather than substantive. It heightens the subjective sense of worth at the expense of objectifying the products of hacking as abstraction. From this containment of the desire for knowledge arises the circular parade of the false problems of discipline and the discipline of false problems.

[069] Only one intellectual conflict has any real bearing on the class issue for hackers: the property question. Whose property is knowledge? Is it the role of knowledge to authorize subjects that are recognized only by their function in an

economy? Or is it the function of knowledge to produce the ever-different phenomena of the hack, in which subjects learn to become other than themselves, and discover the objective world to contain potentials other than as it appears? This is the struggle for knowledge of our time. "The very moment philosophers proclaim ownership of their ideas, they are allying themselves to the powers they are criticizing."*

To hack is to express knowledge in any of its forms. Hacker [070] knowledge implies, in its practice, a politics of free information, free learning, the gift of the result in a peer-to-peer network. Hacker knowledge also implies an ethics of knowledge open to the desires of the productive classes and free from subordination to commodity production. Hacker knowledge is knowledge that expresses the virtuality of nature, by transforming it, fully aware of the bounty and danger. When knowledge is freed from scarcity, the free production of knowledge becomes the knowledge of free producers. This may sound like utopia, but the accounts of actually existing temporary zones of hacker liberty are legion. Stallman: "It was a bit like the garden of Eden. It hadn't occurred to us not to cooperate."*

HACKING

A hack touches the virtual—and transforms the actual. "To [071]
qualify as a hack, the feat must be imbued with innovation, style and technical virtuosity."* The terms hacking and
hacker emerge in this sense in electrical engineering and
computing. As these are leading areas of creative production
in a vectoral world, it is fitting that these names come to
represent a broader activity. The hacking of new vectors of
information has indeed been the turning point in the emergence of a broader awareness of the creative production of
abstraction.

Since its very emergence in computing circles, the hacker [072]
"ethic" has come up against the forces of commodified education and communication. As Himanen writes, hackers,
who "want to realize their passions," present "a general social challenge," but the realization of the value of this challenge "will take time, like all great cultural changes."* And
more than time, for it is more than a cultural change. It will
take struggle, for what the hacker calls into being in the
world is a new world and a new being. Freeing the concept of the hacker from its particulars, understanding it ab-
stractly, is the first step in this struggle.

[073] The apologists for the vectoral interest want to limit the semantic productivity of the term "hacker" to a mere criminality, precisely because they fear its more abstract and multiple potential—its class potential. Everywhere one hears rumors of the hacker as the new form of juvenile delinquent, or nihilist vandal, or servant of organized crime. Or, the hacker is presented as a mere harmless subculture, an obsessive garage pursuit with its restrictive styles of appearance and codes of conduct. Everywhere the desire to open the virtuality of information, to share data as a gift, to appropriate the vector for expression is represented as the object of a moral panic, an excuse for surveillance, and the restriction of technical knowledge to the "proper authorities." This is not the first time that the productive classes have faced this ideological blackmail. The hacker now appears in the official organs of the ruling order alongside its earlier archetypes, the organized worker, the rebellious farmer. The hacker is in excellent company.

[074] The virtual is the true domain of the hacker. It is from the virtual that the hacker produces ever-new expressions of the actual. To the hacker, what is represented as being real is always partial, limited, perhaps even false. To the hacker there is always a surplus of possibility expressed in what is actual, the surplus of the virtual. This is the inexhaustible domain of what is real but not actual, what is not but which may become. The domain where, as Massumi says, "what cannot be experienced cannot but be felt."* To hack is to release the virtual into the actual, to express the difference of the real.

Any domain of nature may yield the virtual. By abstracting [075] from nature, hacking produces the possibility of another nature, a second nature, a third nature, natures to infinity, doubling and redoubling. Hacking discovers the nature of nature, its productive—and destructive—powers. This applies as much in physics as in sexuality, in biology as in politics, in computing as in art or philosophy. The nature of any and every domain may be hacked. It is in the nature of hacking to discover freely, to invent freely, to create and produce freely. But it is not in the nature of hacking itself to exploit the abstractions thus produced.

When the hack is represented in the abstraction of property [076] rights, then information as property creates the hacker class as class. This intellectual property is a distinctive kind of property to land or capital, in that only a qualitatively new creation may lay claim to it. And yet, when captured by the representation of property, the hack becomes the equivalent of any other property, a commodified value. The vectoral class measures its net worth in the same currency as capitalists and pastoralists, making patents and copyrights equivalent to factories or fields.

Through the application of ever-new forms of abstraction, [077] the hacker class produces the possibility of production, the possibility of making something of and with the world— and of living off the surplus produced by the application of abstraction to nature—to any nature. Abstraction, once it starts to be applied, may seem strange, "unnatural," and may bring radical changes in its wake. If it persists, it soon becomes taken for granted. It becomes second nature. Through the production of new forms of abstraction, the hacker class produces the possibility of the future. Of course not every new abstraction yields a productive application to the world. In practice, few innovations ever do so. Yet it can rarely be known in advance which abstractions will mesh with nature in a productive way.

[078] It is in the interests of hackers to be free to hack for hacking's sake. The free and unlimited hacking of the new produces not just "the" future, but an infinite possible array of futures, the future itself as virtuality. Every hack is an expression of the inexhaustible multiplicity of the future, of virtuality. Yet every hack, if it is to be realized as a form of property and assigned a value, must take the form not of an expression of multiplicity, but of a representation of something repeatable and reproducible. Property traps only one aspect of the hack, its representation and objectification as property. It cannot capture the infinite and unlimited virtuality from which the hack draws its potential.

[079] Under the sanction of law, the hack becomes a finite property, and the hacker class emerges, as all classes emerge, out of a relation to a property form. As with land or capital as property forms, intellectual property enforces a relation of scarcity. It assigns a right to a property to an owner at the expense of non-owners, to a class of possessors at the expense of the dispossessed. "The philosophy of intellectual property reifies economic rationalism as a natural human trait."*

By its very nature, the act of hacking overcomes the limits [080] property imposes on it. New hacks supersede old hacks, and devalue them as property. The hack takes information that has been devalued into redundancy by repetition as communication, and produces new information out of it again. This gives the hacker class an interest in the free availability of information rather than in an exclusive right. The immaterial aspect of the nature of information means that the possession by one of information need not deprive another of it. The fields of research are of a different order of abstraction to agricultural fields. While exclusivity of property may be necessary with land, it makes no sense whatsoever in science, art, philosophy, cinema or music.

To the extent that the hack embodies itself in the form of [081] property, it does so in a quite peculiar way, giving the hacker class as a class interests quite different from other classes, be they exploiting or exploited classes. The interest of the hacker class lies first and foremost in a free circulation of information, this being the necessary condition for the renewed expression of the hack. But the hacker class as class also has a tactical interest in the representation of the hack as property, as something from which a source of income may be derived that gives the hacker some independence from the ruling classes. The hacker class opens the virtual into the historical when it hacks a way to make the latter desire a mere particular of the former.

The very nature of the hack gives the hacker a crisis of [082] identity. The hacker searches for a representation of what it is to be a hacker in the identities of other classes. Some see themselves as vectoralists, trading on the scarcity of their property. Some see themselves as workers, but as privileged ones in a hierarchy of wage earners. The hacker class produces itself as itself, but not for itself. It does not (yet) possess a consciousness of its consciousness. It is not aware of its own virtuality. Because of its inability—to date—to become a class for itself, fractions of the hacker class continually split off and come to identify their interests with those of other classes. Hackers run the risk, in particular, of being identified in the eyes of the working and farming classes with vectoralist interests, which seek to privatize information necessary for the productive and cultural lives of all classes.

[083] To hack is to abstract. To abstract is to produce the plane upon which different things may enter into relation. It is to produce the names and numbers, the locations and trajectories of those things. It is to produce kinds of relations, and relations of relations, into which things may enter. Differentiation of functioning components arranged on a plane with a shared goal is the hacker achievement, whether in the technical, cultural, political, sexual or scientific realm. Having achieved creative and productive abstraction in so many other realms, the hacker class has yet to produce itself as its own abstraction. What is yet to be created, as an abstract, collective, affirmative project is, as Ross says, "a hacker's knowledge, capable of penetrating existing systems of rationality that might otherwise seem infallible; a hacker's knowledge, capable of reskilling, and therefore rewriting, the cultural programs and reprogramming the social values

that make room for new technologies; a hacker knowledge, capable also of generating new popular romances around the alternative uses of human ingenuity."*

The struggle of the hacker class is a struggle against itself [084] as much as against other classes. It is in the nature of the hack that it must overcome the hack it identifies as its precursor. A hack only has value in the eyes of the hacker as a qualitative development of a previous hack. Yet the hacker class brings this spirit also into its relation to itself. Each hacker sees the other as a rival, or a collaborator against another rival, not—yet—as a fellow member of the same class with a shared interest. This shared interest is so hard to grasp precisely because it is a shared interest in qualitative differentiation. The hacker class does not need unity in identity but seeks multiplicity in difference.

The hacker class produces distinctions as well as relations, [085] and must struggle against distinctions of its own making in order to reconceive of itself as itself. Having produced itself as the very process of distinction, it has to distinguish between its competitive interest in the hack, and its collective interest in discovering a relation among hackers that expresses an open and ongoing future for its interests. Its competitive interest can be captured in the property form, but its collective interest cannot. The collective interest of the hacker class calls for a new form of class struggle.

The hacker class can enlist those components of other [086] classes that assist in the realization of the hacker class as a class for itself. Hackers have so often provided other classes with the means by which to realize themselves, as the "organic intellectuals" connected to particular class interests and formations. But having guided—and misguided—the working class as its intellectual "vanguard," it is time for hackers to recognize that their interests are separate from those of the working class, but potentially in alliance. It is from the leading edge of the working class that hackers may yet learn to conceive of themselves as a class. If hackers teach workers how to hack, it is workers who teach hackers how to be a class, a class in itself and for itself. The hacker class becomes a class for itself not by adopting the identity of the working class but by differentiating itself from it.

[087] The vectoral puts the overdeveloped world directly in touch with the underdeveloped world, breaching the envelopes of states and communities, even those of the subject itself. The poorest farmers find themselves struggling against not only the local pastoralist class, but against a vectoralist class hell bent on monopolizing the information contained in seed stocks, or the curative properties of medicinal plants long known to traditional peoples. Farmers, workers and hackers confront in its different aspects the same struggle to free information from property, and from the vectoral class. The most challenging hack for our time is to express this common experience of the world.

[088] While not everyone is a hacker, everyone hacks. Touching the virtual is a common experience because it is an experience of what is common. If hacking breaches envelopes, then the great global hack is the movement of the dispossessed of the underdeveloped world, under and over every

border, following every vector toward the promise of the overdeveloped world. The vectors of communication scatter as confetti representations of commodified life around the world, drawing subjects to its objects, turning on vectors of migration on an unprecedented scale. But what remains yet to be hacked is a new opening of expression for this movement, a new desire besides the calling of the representation of the object for its subjects, who will arrive, sooner or later, at boredom and disappointment. The vectoral world is being hacked to bits from the inside and the outside, calling for the combining of all efforts at abstracting desire from property and releasing the properties of abstracted desire.

HISTORY

History is itself an abstraction, hacked out of the recalci- [089]
trant information thrown off by the productive altercations
of presents meshing with pasts. Out of the information expressed by events, history forms orders of objective and subjective representation.

The representation of history dominant in any era is the [090]
product of the educational apparatus established by its ruling powers. Even dissenting history takes form within institutions not of its making. While not all history represents
the interests of the ruling classes, the institution of history
exists as something other than what it can become when
free of class constraint, namely, the abstract guide to transformation of the ruling order in the interests of the producing classes, whose collective action expresses the events history merely represents.

History is not necessity. "History today still designates only [091]
the set of conditions, however recent they may be, from
which one turns away in order to become."* For history
to be something more than a representation, it must seek
something more than its perfection as representation, as an
image faithful to but apart from what it represents. It can express rather its difference from the state of affairs that pres-

ent themselves under the authorship of the ruling class. It can be a history not just of what the world is, but what it can become.

[092] This other history, this hacker history, brings together the record of events as an object apart from collective action with the action of the subjective force that struggles to free itself from its own objectification. Hacker history introduces the productive classes to the product of their own action, which is otherwise presented—not just by the ruling version of history but by the ruling class itself in all its actions—as a thing apart.

[093] Hacker history hacks out of appearances, and returns to the productive classes, their own experience of the containment of their free productive energy in successive property forms. From the direct subjection to an individual owner that is slavery, to the patchwork of local lordships and spiritualized subjection that is feudalism, to the abstract and universalizing private property of the commodified economy, in every era hitherto, a ruling class extracts a surplus from the free capacity of the productive classes. Hacker history not only represents to the productive classes what they have lost, it expresses what they may yet gain—the return of their own productive capacity in and for itself.

[094] The history produced in the institutions of the ruling classes makes history itself into a form of property. To hacker history, the dominant history is but a visible instance of the containment of productive power within representation by the dominant form of property. Even the would-be

"radical" histories, the social histories, the history from be-low, end up as forms of property, traded according to their representational value, in an emerging market for com-modified communication. Critical history only breaks with dominant history when it advances to a critique of its own property form, and beyond, to the expression of a new pro-ductive history and history of the productive.

A hacker history challenges not just the content of history, [095] but its form. Adding yet more representations to the heap of history's goods, even representations of the oppressed and excluded, does nothing if it does not challenge the separa-tion of history as representation from the great productive forces that make history in the first place. The educational apparatus of the overdeveloped world would make even the unscripted voice of the subaltern peasant part of its property, but the productive classes have need only of the speech of their own productivity to recover the productivity of speech.

What matters in the struggle for history is to express its [096] potential to be otherwise, and to make it a part of the pro-ductive resources for the self-awareness of the productive classes themselves, including the hacker class. The hacker class, like productive labor everywhere, can become a class for itself when equipped with a history that expresses its po-tential in terms of the potential of the whole of the dispos-sessed classes.

Hacker history does not need to be invented from scratch, [097] as a fresh hack expressed out of nothing. It quite freely plagiarizes from the historical awareness of all the productive classes of past and present. The history of the free is a free history. It is the gift of past struggles to the present, which carries with it no obligation other than its implementation. It requires no elaborate study. It need be known only in the abstract to be practiced in the particular.

[098] One thing is already known, as part of this gift. The containment of free productivity within the representation of property, as managed by the state in the interests of the ruling class, may accelerate development for a time, but inevitably retards and distorts it in the end. Far from being the perfect form for all time, property is always contingent, and awaits the exceeding of its fetters by some fresh hack. The past weighs like insomnia upon the consciousness of the present.

[099] Production bursts free from the fetters of property, from its local and contingent representations of right and appropriation, and eventually gives rise to an abstract and universalizing form of property, private property. Private property encompasses land, capital, and eventually information, bringing each under its abstract form and making of each a commodity. It cuts land from the continuum of nature and makes of it a thing. It cuts the products made out of nature into objects to be bought and sold and makes of them things also. Finally, private property makes of information, that immaterial potential, a thing. And out of this triple objectification property produces, among other things, its objectified and lifeless brand of history.

[100] The progress of the privatization of property creates at each stage a class who own the means of producing a sur-

plus from it, and a producing class dispossessed of it. This process develops unevenly, but it is possible to abstract from the vicissitudes of events an abstract account of the progress of abstraction, starting with the abstraction of nature that is landed property.

As land becomes the object of a universalizing law of ab-   [101] stracted private property, a class arises who profit from its ownership. The pastoralist class, through its domination of the organs of the state, produces the legal fictions that would legitimate this theft of nature from traditional forms of life.

Secure in its ownership of land, the pastoralist class im-   [102] poses upon the dispossessed whatever form of exploitative relation it can get away with, and get the state to back with force—tenancy, slavery, sharecropping. Each is only the measure of the tolerance of the state for the prerogative of pastoral power. In its thirst for labor that would make land actually productive, and yield a surplus, no indignity is too great, no corner of the world exempt from the claims of property and the uprooting of its custodians.

What makes this dispossession possible is the private prop-   [103] erty hack, by which land emerges as a legal fiction, guaranteeing access to the productivity of nature for the pastoralist class. What accelerates the dispossession of the peasantry is successive agricultural hacks, which increase the productive power of agricultural labor, creating a vast surplus of wealth.

The peasantry, who once held traditional rights in land, find   [104] themselves denied those rights, by a state apparatus in the control of the pastoralist class. The agricultural hack sets flows of dispossessed peasants in motion, and they become, at best, workers, selling their labor to an emerging capitalist class. Thus pastoralism begets capitalism. The pastoral class produces "a social form with distinctive 'laws of motion' that would eventually give rise to capitalism in its mature, industrial form."*

[105]   Just as the pastoralists use the state to secure land as private property, so too the capitalists use their power over the state to secure the legal and administrative conditions for the privatization of flows of raw materials and tools of production in the form of capital. The capitalist class acquires the means to employ labor through the investment of the surplus wealth generated by agriculture and trade in yet more productive abstractions, the product of yet other hacks, which yields the division of labor, the factory system, the engineering of production. The abstractions that are private property, the wage relation and commodity exchange provide a plane upon which the brutal but efficient extraction of a surplus can proceed apace. But without the toil of the great multitude of farmers and workers, and without the ever more inventive hacking of new abstractions, private property alone does not change the world.

[106]   Land and capital for a time represent conflicting interests, struggling against each other through the state for domination. Landed interests try to achieve a monopoly on the sale of foodstuffs within the space of the nation through the state, while capital struggles to open the market and thus push down the price of food. Likewise, pastoralists try to

open the national market to flows of manufactured goods, while capital in its infancy sought to protect its monopoly within the national envelope. This conflict arises out of the difference in the property form based on land as opposed to capital, which are qualitatively different kinds of abstractions.

Capital, the more abstract property form, usually gets the upper hand in its struggle with the pastoral interest and opens the national envelope to cheap primary produce imports. It reduces the amount of the surplus going to the pastoralist class and secures for itself lower costs of production, thus making its goods more competitive internationally. Struggles of this kind are not uncommon among the otherwise allied ruling classes, and are always worth studying in hacker history with an eye for opportunities presented in these moments of transition that the productive classes may turn to their advantage. [107]

The classes that own the means of production, be they a pastoralist class in possession of pastures or farmlands, a capitalist class in possession of factories and forges, or a vectoralist class in possession of stocks, flows and vectors of information, everywhere extract a surplus from the productive classes. The extraction of the surplus is the key to the continuity of class society, but the form of the surplus, and the form of the ruling class itself, passes through three historical phases: pastoralist, capitalist, vectoralist; with their corresponding forms of surplus: rent, profit, margin. As each is based on a more abstract form of property, less and less tied to a particular aspect of the materiality of nature, [108] each is less and less easy to monopolize and secure. Thus each ruling class depends more and more on the force of law to secure its property, making law the dominant superstructural form for preserving an infrastructural power.

[109] Through ownership of the means of production, the ruling classes limit that proportion of the surplus returned to the producing classes, over and above bare subsistence, and return that subsistence in a commodified form. But this does not suffice to dispose of a mounting surplus. The ruling classes must find a market for their produce somewhere. The colonies, where the agricultural surplus is produced, are obliged to buy back their own surplus in the form of manufactured goods.

[110] Capital soon colonizes the culture of its own working class at home, who, struggling to gain some of the surplus they themselves produce, find that they can only cash it in for yet more commodities. The working class of the overdeveloped world becomes the market for what they themselves produce. They find their interests divided from those of the producing classes of the colonies and former colonies. The overdeveloped world becomes overdeveloped by limiting the ability of the underdeveloped world to sell its produce into it, while maintaining its prerogatives over the markets of the underdeveloped world. The overdeveloped world uses the vector at one and the same time to preserve the envelopes of its own states while breaching those of the underdeveloped world. The vector secures the identity of those who shelter within the envelope it maintains by simultaneously puncturing the identity of those subjected to its dislocating effects outside.

In both the developed and the underdeveloped world, the [111] productive classes are induced into identifying their interests with those of the ruling classes, within the envelope of the state.

In the overdeveloped world, the capitalist class and its ju- [112] nior partner, the pastoralist class, secure the consent of the working class through the partial sharing of the surplus, which then gives the working class an interest in preserving the discriminatory vectoral relations that maintain this privilege.

In the underdeveloped world, the pastoralist class and [113] nascent capitalist class secure the support of the predominantly farming producers through the demand for a sovereign state free from colonial rule that can develop autonomously, and for justice in trade with the overdeveloped world. Sovereignty, whether conceded or seized from the overdeveloped world, is not, as the underdeveloped world discovers, enough to secure development. Unequal vectors of trade were and remain the principal cause of exploitation in the underdeveloped world.

The productive classes are so called because they are the [114] real producers of wealth, be they farmers and miners of land, workers of material or immaterial value, or hackers who produce new means of production itself. Their interests and desires do not always coincide of their own accord, which is why they are considered as separate classes, tied to different relations of property, and predominating in different parts of the world. Taken together they have in common their dispossession from the greater part of what they themselves produce. Their history is the history of the struggle to enjoy the fruits of their own labor.

[115] The productive classes may struggle directly against their appropriators, over the terms of the exchange between them, or may struggle indirectly through the state. The state, which the pastoralist and capitalist classes used as an instrument for legitimizing their appropriation of property, can also be the means by which the productive classes seek to resocialize part of the surplus, through the taxation and transfer of the surplus to the productive classes in the form of a social wage, such as health care, education or housing.

[116] Taxation may distribute the surplus toward the producing classes, toward the ruling classes, or may be diverted for the expansion and armament of the state itself. While the ruling class seeks to limit the state's interference in its activities, it also seeks to direct the surplus towards its own uses. Capital may encourage the state to arm itself, and profit by its arming. Here the producing classes end up subsidizing an arrangement between state and capital—the military industrial complex.

[117] Capital usually cedes to the state the information intensive functions that were of benefit to the capitalist and pastoralist classes as a whole, or which are concessions won by the productive classes. The state becomes the manager of the representations through which class society as a whole comes to know and regulate itself. The rise of a vectoralist class put an end to this arrangement. The vectoral class uses the state to extend and defend the privatization of informa-

tion. It attacks the socialized science, culture, communication and education that other ruling classes for the most part left in the hands of the state. "There is an intellectual land grab going on."*

Each ruling class shapes a military force in its own image. [118] The vectoralist class supplants the military industrial complex with the military entertainment complex, where the surplus is directed to the development of vectors for command, control and communication. Where the military industrial complex had socialized part of the risks of new technology for capital and had formed a reliable source of demand for its productive capacity, the military entertainment complex provides these same services to the emergent vectoralist class. The new military ideologies—command and control, the information war, the revolution in military affairs—correspond to the needs and interests of the vectoral class.

At the same time as they privatize what was formerly so- [119] cialized information, the vectoralist class attacks the ability of the hacker class to maintain some degree of autonomy over its working conditions. As the vectoral class comes to monopolize stocks, flows and vectors of information, the hacker class loses its control of its immediate working conditions. The hacker class finds its own ethic of labor compromised, and the agenda for the hack determined by necessities not of its making. The hacker class finds itself sucked into the matrix of the military entertainment complex, hacking out the ways and means of extending the vector as a weapon of mass destruction and a weapon of mass seduction.

[120] Besides its struggle over the value of its labor, and its struggle through the state to reapportion the surplus, each productive class struggles over the autonomy of its working conditions. Farmers form associations, workers form unions. Many seek autonomy through the ownership of some productive tools. The hacker class likewise struggles for autonomy in a world in which the means of production are in the hands of the ruling classes. But the difference is that the hacker class is also a designer of the very tools of production. Hackers program the hardware, software and wetware, and can struggle for tools more amenable to autonomy and cooperation than monopoly and competition.

[121] There is one other struggle that all the productive classes are always engaged in, whether they know it or not. They struggle to exceed the limits to the production of the surplus and its free appropriation imposed as a fetter by the commodity form in general, and by its most restrictive form—private property—in particular. All of the productive classes struggle fitfully to hack temporary zones of liberty out of commodified production and consumption. These struggles have never amounted to much until the development of the vector opened up the possibilities for the theft of information on a grand scale. The productive classes take advantage of the contradictions between the commodification of the vector and the commodification of stocks and flows of information by rival factions of the vectoral class. This is not really theft, but a reappropriation, returning some portion of the popular knowledge and culture of the productive classes to its collective producers.

The commodity form is an abstraction that releases an [122] enormous amount of productive energy, but it does so by diverting production always toward the reproduction of the commodity form. That form becomes a fetter on the free productivity of production itself. The hack is then limited to the hacking of new forms of surplus extraction. This is the most salient point in any history that aims to become a part of the struggle to wrest freedom from necessity.

As land, capital and information are progressively ab- [123] stracted as property, property itself becomes more abstract. Land has a finite and particular form, capital has finite but universal forms, information is both infinite and universal in its potential. The abstraction of property reaches the point where it calls for an abstraction from property. History becomes hacker history when hackers realize that this moment has already arrived.

The class dynamic drives class society to the possibility of [124] overcoming the property form itself, to the overcoming of scarcity and the release of the surplus potential of productivity back into the hands of its producers. What history expresses to the producing classes is this unrealized potential to wrest freedom from necessity as they experience it. Just as property led to the wresting of freedom from natural necessity, the overcoming of the limits to property offers the potential to wrest freedom from the necessities imposed on the productive classes by the constraint of private property, class exploitation and its domination of the state.

A hacker history knows only the present tense. [125]

INFORMATION

Information wants to be free but is everywhere in chains.   [126]

Information is immaterial, but never exists without a mate-   [127]
rial support. Information may be transferred from one material support to another, but cannot be dematerialized—
other than in the more occult of vectoralist ideologies. Information emerges as a concept when it achieves an abstract
relation to materiality. This abstracting of information from
any particular material support creates the very possibility
of a vectoral society, and produces the new terrain of class
conflict—the conflict between the vectoralist and hacker
classes.

Information expresses the potential of potential. When un-   [128]
fettered, it releases the latent capacities of all things and
people, objects and subjects. Information is the plane upon
which objects and subjects come into existence as such. It is
the plane upon which the potential for the existence of new
objects and subjects may be posited. It is where virtuality
comes to the surface.

The potential of potential that information expresses has its   [129]
dangers. But its enslavement to the interests of the vectoral

class poses greater dangers still. When information is free, it is free to act as a resource for the averting of its own dangerous potentials. When information is not free, then the class that owns or controls it turns its capacity toward its own interest and away from information's own inherent virtuality.

[130] Information exceeds communication. Deleuze: "We do not lack communication. On the contrary, we have too much of it. We lack creation. We lack resistance to the present."* Information is at once this resistance, and what it resists—its own dead form, communication. Information is both repetition and difference. Information is representation, in which difference is the limit to repetition. But information is also expression, in which difference exceeds repetition. The hack turns repetition into difference, representation into expression, communication into information. Property turns difference into repetition, freezing free production and distributing it as a representation. Property, as representation, fetters information.

[131] The enabling conditions for freedom of information do not stop at the "free" market, no matter what the apologists for the vectoral class may say. Free information is not a product, but a condition of the effective allocation of resources. The multiplicity of public and gift economies, a plurality of forms—keeping open the property question—is what makes free information possible.

[132] The commodification of information means the enslavement of the world to the interests of those whose margins depend on information's scarcity, the vectoral class. The many potential benefits of free information are subordi-

nated to the exclusive benefits in the margin. The infinite virtuality of the future is subordinated to the production and representation of futures that are repetitions of the same commodity form.

The subordination of information to the repetition of communication means the enslavement of its producers to the interests of its owners. It is the hacker class that taps the virtuality of information, but it is the vectoralist class that owns and controls the means of production of information on an industrial scale. Their interests lie in extracting as much margin as possible from information, in commodifying it to the nth degree. Information that exists solely as private property is no longer free, for it is chained to the repetition of the property form. [133]

The interests of hackers are not always totally opposed to those of the vectoral class. There are compromises to be struck between the free flow of information and extracting a flow of revenue to fund its further development. But while information remains subordinated to ownership, it is not possible for its producers to freely calculate their interests, or to discover what the true freedom of information might potentially produce in the world. The stronger the hacker class alliance with the other producing classes, the less it has to answer the vectoralist imperative. [134]

Information may want to be free, but it is not possible to know the limits or potentials of its freedom when the virtual is subordinated to this actual state of ownership and scarcity. Privatizing information and knowledge as commodified "content" distorts and deforms its free develop- [135]

ment, and prevents the very concept of its freedom from its own free development. "As our economy becomes increasingly dependent on information, our traditional system of property rights applied to information becomes a costly fetter on our development."* The subordination of hackers to the vectoralist interest means the enslavement not only of the whole of human potential, but also natural potential. While information is chained to the interests of its owners, it is not just hackers who may not know their interests, no class may know what it may become.

[136] Information in itself is mere possibility. It requires an active capacity to become productive. But where knowledge is dominated by the education of the ruling classes, it produces the capacity to use information for the purposes of producing and consuming within the limits of the commodity. This produces a mounting desire for information that meets the apparent lack of meaning and purpose in life. The vectoralist class fills this need with communication that offers these desires a mere representation and objectification of possibility.

[137] For everyone to become free to join in the virtuality of knowledge, information and the capacity to grasp it must be free also, so that all classes may have the potential to hack for themselves and their kind a new way of life. The condition for this liberation is the abolition of a class rule that imposes scarcity on knowledge, and indeed on virtuality itself.

[138] Free information must be free in all its aspects—as a stock, as a flow, and as a vector. The stock of information is the

raw material out of which history is abstracted. The flow of information is the raw material out of which the present is abstracted, a present that forms the horizon that the abstract line of an historical knowledge crosses, indicating a future in its sights. Neither stocks nor flows of information exist without vectors along which they may be actualized. Even so, it is not enough that these elements are brought together as a representation that may then be shared freely. The spatial and temporal axes of free information must do more than offer a representation of things, as a world apart. They must become the means of coordination of the expression of a movement capable of connecting the objective representation of things to the presentation of a subjective action.

Information, when it is truly free, is free not for the purpose of representing the world perfectly, but for expressing its difference from what is, and for expressing the cooperative force that transforms what is into what may be. The sign of a free world is not the liberty to consume information, or to produce it, nor even to implement its potential in private worlds of one's choosing. The sign of a free world is the liberty for the collective transformation of the world through abstractions freely chosen and freely actualized.

[139]

NATURE

The hack expresses the nature of nature as its difference [140] from itself—or at least its difference from its representation. The hack expresses the virtuality of nature and nature as the virtuality of expression.

Nature appears as a representation at the point at which [141] what the representation designates disappears. Once collective agency has begun to wrest a portion of freedom from necessity, then nature in itself, as pure, unmediated experience, appears as the inaccessible object of a longing. Nature appears as precious and elusive, always just out of reach. It becomes the highest value, treasured for its very inaccessibility. Contending forces wield it as a weapon in the struggle for the hearts and minds of a vectoral people, a people that desire a nature that it persuades itself can only be had for a price. Nature becomes a sign at stake in the class struggle.

Nature seized as property makes of it a thing that can be [142] appropriated as a value. The property form turns nature into an object and its appropriator into a subject. Or so it appears in the representation that is the property relation. Property produces the appearance of separation from nature. Property produces the representation of a world that is "socially constructed," by separating subjective possession from the object possessed.

[143] Through collective action, the productive classes wrest freedom from necessity, in the form of a transformed nature, a second nature, more amenable to existence. The transformation of nature into second nature frees human existence from necessity, but creates new forms of necessity. Nietzsche: "Every victorious second nature will become a first nature."* Thus is produced the appearance of the necessity of necessity, which is really no more than the appearance of appearance.

[144] In the creation of a collective existence, in culture, society, economy and polity, collective agency alienates itself from nature, and nature from itself. It becomes the creator of its own nature, if not consciously, then at least collectively. Only by apprehending this collective nature consciously, can the nature against which agency shapes itself be embraced in its difference. Nature "works"—on itself and against itself. Producing the difference that is its difference.

[145] Nature seized as property becomes a resource for the creation of a second nature of commodified objects. History becomes an endless "development" in which nature is seized as an object, and made over in the form that suits a particular subjective interest. But because subjective interest is hitherto a class interest, a property interest, the transformation of nature into second nature produces freedom from necessity only for the ruling class and its favorites. For subordinate classes, it produces new necessities.

Class society, our second nature, becomes so natural that [146] nature itself comes to be represented in its terms. Class is represented as what is natural; nature is represented as if it were just like class society. As with every representation, this double displacement is a play of the false, and in this case, is a productive falsification of the false. Only the recovery of the history of class society, as the transformation of nature into second nature in the image of commodified competition, makes possible a recovery of the nature of nature, as itself a history which encompasses this class history, but does not of necessity conform to its representation, nor of necessity impose its inevitability on history.

Neither the appropriators of nature in the form of prop- [147] erty, nor the dispossessed who struggle for public property as compensation for their dispossession, have an immediate interest in nature as nature. Theirs is a struggle over second nature. Nature itself disappears in its transformation. It reappears as a limit to its endless exploitation only to the extent that it is appropriated as property. It reappears to both exploiting and producing classes as an inventory of property running out. But while the exploiting classes, whose rule is based on property, have no option but to see nature as property, and thus as limit, the producing classes express, in their productive nature, nature's own productivity, if only it could be freed from its representation as a thing exploited to the point of scarcity.

The subordinate classes of the overdeveloped world dis- [148] cover an interest in nature's preservation at the point at which the development of second nature has in some degree freed them from nature's necessities. But this discovery of an interest in nature puts the subordinate classes of the overdeveloped world at odds with those of the underdeveloped world, for whom nature is still in the process of disappearance, and still appears as grim necessity. Property produces both the appearance of the scarcity of nature for some, and the scarcity of second nature for others; the necessity of arresting second nature for some; the necessity of accelerating it for others. The producing classes as a whole can only reconcile their interests by freeing nature from the grip of property, which is what actually divides them.

[149] Nature knows no objects, no subjects, and no representation. Its appearance in representation as object or subject is a false appearance. Yet it is only in its falsity that it can be apprehended in class society, which produces the relation between nature and second nature as an objectified relation. But to rediscover nature as difference, rather than falsity, requires the transformation of a world capable of sustaining itself only by objectifying nature.

[150] To the extent that nature exists even in its disappearance, it exists as expression. Nature still exists, not as the other of the social, but as the multiplicity of forces that the human in concert with the nonhuman articulate and express. In differentiating itself from nature, human agency does not alienate itself from nature, it merely brings into being yet one more aspect of nature's multiplicity. Rectifying the exploitation of nature does not mean a return to a representation of it prior to its transformation, which can only appear as a false image, as it too is produced by the very transformation expe-

rienced as alienating. Rather, out of the multiplicity of natures, collective human agency can join its productive energies with those that affirm nature's own productivity. "We are not in the world, we become with the world."*

The representation of nature as God's estate, as the engine [151] of competition, as complex data networks—all of these abstractions of nature abolish it in their representation of it, and yet are partial expressions of its multiplicity. Education teaches the model of nature that corresponds to the property form of the day—land, capital, information. Each appears as more true than the last at the point at which the form of property from which it derives has become second nature. As each representation of property installs itself in the world, falsifying the world itself in its image, it falsifies the previous false representation of nature—and validates as true the one that mirrors it back in its own mirror. Liberating nature from its representation is the liberation of knowledge from education, which is to say, from property.

To the hacker, nature is another name for the virtual. It is [152] another way of representing the unrepresentable multiplicity from which the hack expresses its ever-renewable forms. There is an interest that the hacker class has in nature, but it is not in a representation of nature's "harmony," that nostalgia that may be comfortably indulged in overdeveloped world. The hacker interest is in another nature altogether, in a nature expressing the limitless multiplicity of things. This is the nature from which any and every hack derives. The hacker interest in nature is not in its scarcity, but in its multiplicity.

[153] In the overdeveloped world, the total transformation of nature into second nature does more than complete the disappearance of nature as nature and lead to its return as the representation of what desire lacks. The transformation of nature into second nature becomes the transformation of second nature into third nature. This latter-day transformation is driven in no small part by the desire to reconstitute nature at least as an image of a lost desire. Third nature appears as the totality of images and stories that provide for second nature a context, an environment, within which it comes to represent itself as the spectacle of a natural order.

[154] Once the vector reaches the point of the development of telesthesia—the perception at a distance of the telegraph, telephone, television—it effects a separation of the flow of communication from the flow of objects and subjects, and thus produces the appearance of information as a world apart. Information—in the commodified form of communication—becomes the governing metaphor for the world precisely because it dominates it in actuality. Third nature emerges, as did second nature, out of the representation of nature as property. Seized as information, not merely as physical resource, the genetic makeup of the whole biosphere can become property, be it as public or private property. This may indeed be the last frontier in the struggle to appropriate the world as a resource. This appropriation is no less false and partial than its predecessors. It is an illusory reality that conforms to the real illusion of property in our time.

Third nature, in its very totality, its spectacle of vectors and [155]
vectors of spectacle, becomes an ecology of images which
may yet become an image of a possible ecology. Third nature relentlessly enfolds the subject in images of the world
as its object. But in its very ubiquity, it dissolves the particular relations of subjects to objects, and represents subjects as
a whole with the image of an objective world as a whole. In
its very falsity, it represents the relation between subject and
object as a false relation, but nevertheless as a relation. Third
nature reveals its own nature to be something produced.

Third nature reveals itself as something not only produced, [156]
but productive. Information appears as expression, not just
as representation, as something produced in its difference
from the world. The world appears as something produced
through the expression of collective action. Third nature
may come into existence to render quantities of objects to
subjects as if they were qualities, but it ends up revealing the
qualitative production of production itself. Or at least, this
virtuality hovers over third nature as its promise. There may
be no return to nature, but as third nature extends itself in
time and space, it becomes the medium of expression of the
production of a fourth nature, a fifth—nature to infinity—
natures which may overcome the destructive limits of the
second nature produced by class society.

P R O D U C T I O N

Production meshes objects and subjects, breaking their en-   [157]
velopes, blurring their identities, blending each into new formation. Representation struggles to keep up, to reassign objective and subjective status to the products of production.
Production is the repetition of the construction and deconstruction of objectivity and subjectivity in the world.

Hacking is the production of production. The hack pro-   [158]
duces a production of a new kind, which has as its result a
singular and unique product, and a singular and unique producer. Every hacker is at one and the same time producer
and product of the hack, and emerges as a singularity that is
the memory of the hack as process.

The hack as pure hack, as pure production of production,   [159]
expresses as a singular instance the multiplicity of the nature
out of which and within which it moves as an event. Out of
the singular event of the hack comes the possibility of its
representation, and out of its representation comes the possibility of its repetition as production and its production as
repetition.

The representation and repetition of the singular hack as a   [160]
typical form of production takes place via its appropriation

by and as property. The recuperation of the hack for production takes the form of its representation to and within the social as property. But the hack, in and of itself, is always distinct from its appropriation for commodity production. Production takes place on the basis of a prior hack that gives to production its formal, social, repeatable and reproducible form. Every production is a hack formalized and repeated on the basis of its representation as property. To produce is to repeat; to hack, to differentiate. If production is the hack captured by property and repeated, the hack is production produced as something other than itself.

[161]   Production transforms nature into objective and subjective elements that form an ensemble, in which a second nature emerges. This second nature consists of a sociality of objects and subjects that may enter into relations of production for the further, quantitative, development as second nature. The appearance of a distinction between the natural and the social, the objective and the subjective, is what production based on property produces and reproduces as abstraction.

[162]   The qualitative transformation of second nature requires the production of production, or the intervention of the hack. The degree of dynamism or openness of a state is directly proportional to its capacity to hack. The hack overcomes the distinction between object and subject, the natural and the social, opening a space for free production that is not marked in advance by the properties of commodification. The hack is at one and the same time the force that opens toward increasing the surplus, and something deeply

threatening to any fixed, fast-frozen relations. Not many states can maintain conditions in which the hack thrives, even as they come to recognize its power. The hack always appears to policy makers as a problem, even for the most abstract of states.

A state that develops the hack as a form of intellectual [163] property will at one and the same time experience rapid growth in its productive capacity, but also in its qualitative capacity for transformation and differentiation. Such a state develops second nature to its limit, but contains within itself the seeds of its own overcoming, once the hack frees itself from property's artifice of limits and limits of artifice. This is the endless anxiety of the vectoral class: that the very virtuality they depend on, that uncanny capacity of the hacker class to mint new properties for commodification, threatens to hack into existence new forms of production beyond commodification, beyond class rule.

The hack produces both a useful and a useless surplus. The [164] useful surplus goes into expanding the realm of freedom wrested from necessity. The useless surplus is the surplus of freedom itself, the margin of free production unconstrained by production for necessity. As the surplus in general expands, so too does the possibility of expanding its useless portion, out of which the possibility of hacking beyond the existing forms of property will arise.

The production of a surplus creates the possibility of the [165] expansion of freedom from necessity. Marx: "The true realm of freedom, the development of human powers as an end in itself, begins beyond it, though it can only flourish with this realm of necessity as its basis."* But in class society, the production of a surplus also creates new necessities. Surplus producing societies may be free societies, or they may be subject to domination by a ruling class or coalition of ruling classes. What calls for explanation are the means by which successive ruling classes capture the surplus and turn it away from free production, and toward the reproduction and repetition of class rule.

[166] Class domination takes the form of the capture of the productive potential of society and its harnessing to the production, not of liberty, but of class domination itself. The ruling class subordinates the hack to forms of production that advance class power, and the suppression or marginalisation of other forms of hacking.

[167] When the pastoralist class dominates, it is indifferent to any hack that develops non-agricultural production. Production remains land based and dedicated to the valorization of land. When the capitalist class dominates, it frees the hack for the production of new forms of useful production, but it subordinates the hack to the accumulation of capital. Hacking that leads to the production of new types of consumable object and consuming subject are the only kind not marginalized. So while the capitalist class provides resources and encouragement for the nascent hacker class, it is under the condition of subordination to commodification. When the vectoralist class dominates, it frees the hack for the production of many kinds of useless production, and thus is often seen as an ally of the hacker class. The vectoralist class act only out of self-interest, for they extract their margin

from the commodification, not just of production, but of the production of production. Their goal is the commodification of the hack itself.

Under pastoralist or capitalist rule, the free and useless [168] hack is suppressed or marginalized, but otherwise retains its own gift economy. Under vectoralist rule, the hack is actively encouraged and courted, but only under the sign of commodified production. For the hacker, the tragedy of the former is to be neglected, of the latter, not to be neglected.

Whether in its pastoralist, capitalist or vectoralist phases, [169] commodity production stages again and again a struggle within its ruling class between that fraction which owns the means of production directly and that fraction which can control it indirectly through the accumulation of money with which to finance it. The power of finance is an abstract and abstracting power, quantifying and objectifying the world, directing resources from one development to another with increasing speed. The development of finance is inseparable from the development of the vector of telesthesia, which frees flows of quantitative and qualitative information from any specific location. Finance is that aspect of the development of the vector that represents its objectifying power in the world. But while finance acquires ever-greater velocity and viscosity as the vector develops, it always depends on finding a productive outlet for its investments. If the ruling class is a vampire, finance is the vampire's vampire.

Production produces not only the object as commodity, but [170] also the subject who appears as its consumer, even though it is actually its producer. Under vectoralist rule, society becomes indeed a "social factory" which makes subjects as much as objects out of the transformation of nature into second nature. "Laboring processes have moved outside the factory walls to invest the entire society."* The capitalist class profits from the producing class as producer of objects. The vectoralist class profits from the producing class as consumer of its own subjectivity in commodified form.

[171] The producers of commodities, be they farmers turning the earth, or workers turning the lathe or the page, are themselves all products of production. As the production of objects becomes complex and manifold, so too does subjectivity. Lukács: "This fragmentation of the object of production necessarily entails the fragmentation of its subject. In consequence of the rationalization of the work-process the human qualities and idiosyncrasies of the worker appear increasingly as mere sources of error."* As the work process extends beyond the factory to the whole of life, so too does this production of the fragmented subject. Whole new industries then arise promising therapies and diversions and miracle cures to make this aberrant subject whole again, including political miracle cures promising to reunite the subject within its envelope by abolishing the vectoral complexities of production. Hacking cannot be a return to this imaginary wholeness of being, but it can open toward the becoming of the virtual.

[172] Production that produces subjects as if they were objects produces also its own—temporary—return of a free productivity beyond the vectoral subject. Since the great upheavals of 1989 in the south and the east, the world is periodically

swept up in weird global media events, in which movements grasp their moment, taking over the streets, and through capture of symbolic space capture also moments of media time, in which to demonstrate to the world that another life is possible. Whether in Beijing or Berlin, Seattle or Seoul, Genoa or Johannesburg, the productive classes come momentarily to the same conclusion. Guattari: "The only acceptable finality for human activity is the production of a subjectivity that is auto-enriching its relation to the world in a continuous fashion."* What calls for a creative application of the hack is the production of new vectors along which the event may continue to unfold after its initial explosion into social space, and avoid capture by representation.

What the farming, working and hacking classes have in common is an interest in abstracting production from its subordination to ruling classes who turn production into the production of new necessities, who wrest slavery from surplus. What the farming and working classes lack in a direct knowledge of free production the hacking class has from direct experience. What the hacking class lacks is the depths of an historic class memory of revolt against alienated production. This the farming and working classes have in spades. [173]

Having produced the surplus out of which free productivity may yet be hacked, it remains only to combine the objective existence of the working and farming classes with the subjective capacity of the hacker class to produce production as free production. The elements of a free productivity exist already in an atomized form, in the productive classes. [174]

What remains is the release of its virtuality. The vectoralist class knows this, and does its best to reduce productivity to property, information to communication, expression to representation, nature to necessity.

[175] The vectoralist class puts its snout into the trough of the surplus on the basis of an ever more abstract, and hence more flexible, form of property than the pastoralist or capitalist class. Zizek: "the thing can only survive as its own excess."* But property also presents it with a problem that threatens its existence. So-called intellectual property is property that not merely has a separate legal existence to other property, but is different in kind. Land need only occupy different space to other land, capital's property likewise need only be distinct in space and time. The vectoralist class depends on the hacker class to produce the qualitative differences of intellectual property that it comes directly to own, and indirectly to profit by, and the owner of the vectors of its distribution. It depends on the very class capable of hacking into actuality the very virtuality it must control to survive.

P R O P E R T Y

Property is theft!" as Proudhon says.* It is theft abstracted, [176] the theft of nature from itself, by collective social labor, constrained within the property form. Property is not naturally occurring. It is not a natural right but an historical product, product of a powerful hack of ambivalent consequences. To make something property is to separate it from a continuum, to mark it or bound it, to represent it as something finite. At the same time, making something as property connects it, via a representation of it as a separate and finite object, to the subject who owns it. What is cut from one process joins another process, what was nature becomes second nature.

Property founds bourgeois subjectivity, the subjectivity of [177] the owner. But it also founds subaltern subjectivity, the subjectivity of the non-owner. Property founds subjectivity as the relation between possession and nonpossession. Property forms the logic of self-interest within the envelope of the subject just as it forms the logic of class interest within the envelope of the state.

When a relation is produced as a relation of property, then [178] the things designated within that relation become comparable as if in the same terms and on the same plane. Property is the syntax of an abstract plane upon which all things may be things with one quality in common, the quality of property. This abstraction, in which things are detached from their expression, represented as objects, and attached via their representations to a new expression, makes the world over in its image, as a world made for and by property. It appears as if property forms the ways and means of nature itself, when it is merely the ways and means of the second nature of class rule.

[179] Traditional property forms are local and contingent. Modern, or vectoral property is abstract and universal. With the demise of feudalism property becomes an abstract relation, and the conflict property generates also becomes abstract. It becomes class conflict. Owners of property arise, and range their interests against non-owners. As the abstract property form evolves to incorporate first land, then capital, then information, both owners and non-owners are brought face to face with the possibilities of class alliance as well as conflict. But just as property cuts through other stakes in conflict, so too does ownership or non-ownership of private property abstract and simplify the grounds of conflict, in the form of the contention between the owning and non-owning classes.

[180] The conflicts upon which the development of the vectoral world hinges become conflicts over property, and thus class conflict: Conflict over the form of property, the ownership of property, over the surplus produced via property, over the limits to the property relation per se. The division of property, the abstraction of things as property, produces conflict by producing the separation of subjects and objects, and as-

signing objects to some subjects over others, and hence the separation of one expression of subjectivity from another. Identity is the subject representing itself to itself as the properties it desires but lacks.

Property comes in many forms, and there are antagonisms [181] between these forms, and yet one form of property may be exchanged for another, as all forms of property belong to the same abstract plane. Vectoral property is a plane on which the object confronts those subjects either belonging to, or excluded from, its possession. Conflict between classes becomes the struggle to transform one form of property into another. The ruling classes fight to turn all property from which they might extract a surplus into private property. The productive classes struggle to collectivize the property upon which the reproduction of their existence depends, via the state. The ruling classes then struggle again to privatize this social component of property. "Liberty" and "Efficiency" versus "Justice" and "Security" becomes the form in which the class struggle represents itself as a struggle over the merits of rival kinds of property. Only in vectoral society are there riots over pension plans.

The conflict between private and public property advances [182] into each domain that property claims as its own. As property claims more and more of the world, more and more of the world construes its interests and being in terms of property. The struggle over property goes to first one class or class alliance then the other, but property is only entrenched as the form in which the struggle is conducted. As property itself becomes more and more abstract, so too does the embedding of history in the property form and of the property form in history.

[183]   Land is the primary form of property. The privatization of land that is a productive asset as property gives rise to a class of interest among its owners. These owners are the pastoralist class. Pastoralists acquire land as private property through the forced dispossession of peasants who traditionally share a portion of the commons. These peasants, who once enjoyed reciprocal rights with their feudal lords, find themselves "free"—from any right at all. They are free to be exploited as farmers, but also find themselves in many parts of the world violently expropriated, enslaved, indentured— exploited.

[184]   The exploitation of the landless farmer is a crude, violent and wasteful business, when the farmer is not given incentive to work land efficiently. But when the farmer has an interest in productivity, necessitated by one property relation or another, but most usually as a freeholder who must pay the pastoralist rent, then the increasing extraction of a surplus is possible. This is the surplus on the back of which the history of all other productions takes place.

[185]   The instrument of rent puts land into play as a form of property that has a degree of abstraction inherent in it. All land becomes comparable on the basis of this abstract plane of property. However, land is in more or less fixed supply, and by definition is fixed in place, so the abstracting of land as property is limited. Land is a form of property particularly subject to the formation of monopoly. The owners of the best lands face no effective competition, land be-

ing ultimately in fixed supply. They gradually extend their ownership, and thus their ability to monopolize the surplus through the extraction of rents, if not held in check by resort to the powers of the state by other classes.

Capital is the secondary form of property. The privatization [1.86] of productive assets in the form of tools and machines and also of working materials gives rise to a class of interest among its owners, the capitalist class. Dispossessed peasants, with nothing to sell but their capacity to work, create this vast stock of capital as private property for the capitalist class, and in so doing create a power over and against themselves. They are paid in wages, but the return that accrues to the owners of capital as property is called profit.

The instrument of profit puts capital into play as a form of [1.87] property that has a greater degree of abstraction inherent in it than that of land. All physical resources now become comparable on the basis of this abstract plane of property. However, capital, unlike land, is not in fixed supply or disposition. It can be made and remade, moved, aggregated, dispersed. A much greater degree of potential can be released from the world as a productive resource once the abstract plane of property includes both land and capital. Where the value of land arises in part out of natural scarcity, the scarcity of things made by productive industry requires the abstraction of property as an artifice to maintain and reproduce scarcity. The possibility of revolt against scarcity arises for the first time at this point in the abstraction of property.

Capital as property also gives rise to a class interest among [1.88] its owners, sometimes opposed, sometimes allied, to that of pastoralists. Capital threw its political energies into the over-throw of the patchwork feudal class relations, but also found itself sometimes opposed to the pastoralist class that consol-idated the feudal property system into the abstraction of land. What capital opposed was the pastoralist ability to ex-ploit its monopoly over land rent to secure the lion's share of the surplus. Capitalist and pastoralist interests struggle over the partition of the surplus between rent and profit. The pastoralist has the natural monopoly of land, but cap-ital usually prevails, as it has a greater capacity for abstrac-tion.

[189]   History makes a qualitative leap when the capitalist class liberates itself from the fetter of the pastoralist interest. The capitalist class recognizes the value of the hack in the abstract, whereas the pastoralists were slow to appreciate the productivity that can flow from the application of ab-straction to the production process. Under the influence of capital, the state sanctions nascent forms of intellectual property, such as patents and copyrights, that secure an inde-pendent existence for hackers as a class, and a flow of inno-vations in culture and science from which history issues. Capital represents private property to itself as if it is natural, but comes to appreciate the artificial extension of property into new, productive forms under the impact of the hack.

[190]   Information, once it becomes a form of property, develops beyond a mere support for capital and for a pastoralist class belatedly aware of the value of increased productivity for its rent rolls. It becomes the basis of a form of accumulation in its own right. Just as farmers and workers find themselves

confronting a class owning the means of production, so too hackers find themselves confronting a new class of owners, in this case of the means of producing, storing and distributing information—the vectoralist class. The vectoralist class struggles first to establish its monopoly over information—a far more abstract form of property than land or capital—and then to establish its power over the other ruling classes. It secures as much of the surplus as it can as margin—the return on ownership of information—at the expense of profit and rent.

Viewed from the current stage of historical development, [191] each of these ruling classes appears to develop out of the productivity of the hack. The pastoralist class develops out of the productivity of private land ownership, a legal hack. The capitalist class develops out of the productivity, not just of private property, but of technical innovations in power and machinery. The vectoralist class develops out of further technical innovations in communication and control. Each in turn competes with its predecessor. Each competes for the capacity to extract as much of the surplus of total productivity as possible for its own accumulation. Each struggles with the productive classes over the disposition of the surplus. But that there is an ever-expanding surplus to struggle over is the product of the application of the hacker's abstraction to the invention of new forms of production, or new desires for consumption, all within the framework of property.

Those dispossessed by the capture of a resource by prop- [192] erty come to conceive of their interests in terms of property. They may struggle individually to become owners of it, or they may struggle collectively to reappropriate a portion of it. Either way, property becomes the stake in the struggle for the producing classes as much as for the property owning classes.

[193] Land, capital and information all appear as domains of struggle between possessors defending or extending the claim of private property, and the dispossessed, who struggle to extend or defend public property. Farmers struggle against their landlessness. Workers struggle against their dispossession, to claim a social wage. Hackers struggle to socialize a portion of the information stocks, flows and vectors on which the hack depends.

[194] The hacker class, which has some sliver of ownership conferred on it by the instrument of intellectual property, finds its rights challenged again and again by vectoralist interests. Hackers, like farmers and workers before them, find that their ownership of the immediate tools of production is compromised both by the market power of the possessing class confronting them, but also by the influence that class can have over the state's definition of the representations of property. Thus hackers as individuals are obliged to sell out their interests, and hackers as a class find their property rights diminished.

[195] Hackers must calculate their interests not as owners, but as producers, for this is what distinguishes them from the vectoralist class. Hackers do not merely own, and profit by owning information. They produce new information, and as producers need access to it free from the absolute domina-

tion of the commodity form. If what defines the activity of hacking is that it is a free productivity, an expression of the virtuality of nature, then its subjection to private property and the commodity form is a fetter upon it. "When the meaning of a string of characters can be bought and locked into place this is the thermodynamics of language reduced to a single cryogenic chamber."*

That hackers as a class have an interest in information as [196] private property can blind the hacker class to the dangers of too strong an insistence on the protection of that property. Any small gain the hacker gets from the privatization of information is compromised by the steady accumulation of the means of realizing its value in the hands of the vector-alist class. Since information is crucial to the hack itself, the privatization of information is not in the interests of the hacker class. To maintain their autonomy, hackers need some means of extracting an income from the hack, and thus from some limited protection of their rights. Since information is an input as well as an output of the hack, this interest has to be balanced against a larger interest in the free distribution of all information. In the short term, some form of intellectual property may secure some autonomy for the hacker class from the vectoralist class, but in the long term, the hacker class realizes its virtuality through the abolition of intellectual property as a fetter on the hack itself. The hacker class frees the hack by hacking class itself, realizing itself by abolishing itself.

Where the farmer suffered the enclosure of the pastoral [197] commons, the hacker must resist the enclosure of the information commons. Where workers struggled to make public some portion of the surplus as social security, so too hackers must define a portion of the surplus as cultural and scientific security. Hacking as a pure, free experimental activity must be free from any constraint that is not self imposed. Only out of its liberty will it hack the means of producing a surplus of liberty and liberty as a surplus. But like the farmers' and workers' movements, hackers may decide to pursue a radical or reformist politics, and will redefine what is radical and what is reformist as it reclaims the common interest in what in the jargon of the vectoralist class is merely "intellectual property."

[198] Without an information commons, all classes become captives of the vectoralist privatization of education. This is an interest the hacker shares with farmers and workers, who demand the public provision of education. Hackers, farmers and workers also have a common interest in an information commons with which to maintain a vigilant eye on the state, which is all too often subject to ruling class capture. Even the pastoralist and capitalist classes can sometimes be allies in limiting the subjection of information by the vectoralist class to commodification. The vectoralist interest grasps at a monopoly power over information, and puts monopolizing the surplus ahead of the expansion of the surplus. What is "efficient" for the vectoralist class may impede the development of the surplus, and thus the virtuality of history.

[199] The hacker class must think tactically about property, balancing public and private property in the scales of class interest and class alliance, but in the knowledge that the privatization of information is not in its long term interest

as a class. Part of its strategy may be the enlistment of other classes in an alliance for the public production of information. But another strategy may be to extend another kind of property altogether—the property that is the gift.

Both the private and public forms of property are property [200] in which subjects confront objects as buyers and sellers, via the quantitative medium of money. Even public property does not alter this quantification. The commodity economy, be it public or private, commodifies its subjects as well as its objects and sets a limit on the virtuality of nature.

Private property arose in opposition not only to feudal [201] property, but also to traditional forms of the gift economy, which are a fetter to the increased productivity of the commodity economy. Money is the medium through which land, capital, information and labor all confront each other as abstract entities, reduced to an abstract plane of measurement. Qualitative exchange is superseded by quantified, monetized exchange. The gift as property is pure qualitative exchange. The gift becomes a marginal form of property, everywhere invaded by the commodity, and turned towards mere consumption. The gift is marginal, but nevertheless plays a vital role in cementing reciprocal and communal relations among people who otherwise can only confront each other as buyers and sellers of commodities.

As production develops into its vectoralized form, the [202] means appear for the renewal of the gift economy. The vectoral form of relation allows for an abstraction of qualitative exchange that may become as vast and powerful as that of quantitative exchange. Everywhere that the vector reaches, it brings into the orbit of the commodity. But everywhere the vector reaches, it also brings with it the possibility of the "opening of the dimension of the gift, its grace or beauty, between the precious and the gratis, between the unique and the ordinary."*

[203] The hacker class has a close affinity with the gift economy. The hacker struggles to produce a subjectivity that is qualitative and singular, in part through the act of the hack itself, but only in part. The hack reveals to the hacker the qualitative, open and virtual dimension of the hacker's immersion in nature, but it does not reveal the hacker as hacker to other hackers, or to the world. The hack reveals the non-subjective surplus of subjectivity, just as it reveals the non-objective surplus of objectivity.

[204] The gift, as a qualitative exchange, creates singular producers and production as singularity. The gift expresses the virtuality of the production of production, whereas commodified property represents the producer as an object, a quantifiable commodity like any other, of relative value only. The gift of information need not give rise to conflict over information as property, for information need not suffer the artifice of scarcity.

[205] The gift relation of vectoralized information makes possible, for the first time since the dawn of the vectoral world, a new abstraction of nature. Nature need not be objectified. It need not appear as something separate from its subjects in a relationship of ownership or non-ownership. Nature appears in its qualitative, rather than quantitative aspect. The

unsustainable paradox of limitless productivity based on scarcity, both natural and unnatural, need not run on and on to its seemingly inevitable fall. Within the gift relation, nature appears as endlessly productive in its differences, in its qualitative, not its quantitative aspect. The possibility emerges of putting nature's finite resources to work for the virtuality of difference, rather than for objectification and quantification. The latter finally appear as partial abstractions, as falling short of the abstraction of abstraction. If property is theft, then it is theft, in the first instance, from nature. The gift has the capacity to return nature as itself to itself.

The vectoralist class contributes, unwittingly, to the development of the vectoral world within which the gift as the limit to property could return, but soon recognizes its error. As the vectoral economy develops, less and less of it takes the form of a public space of open and free gift exchange, and more and more of it takes the form of commodified production for private sale. The vectoralist class can grudgingly accommodate some margin of public information, as the price it pays to the state for the furtherance of its main interests. But the vectoralist class quite rightly sees in the gift a challenge not just to its profits but to its very existence. The gift economy is the virtual proof for the parasitic and superfluous nature of vectoralists as a class. [206]

REPRESENTATION

The politics of information, the history of knowledge, advance not through a critical negation of false representations but a positive hacking of the virtuality of expression. Representation always mimics but is less than what it represents; expression always differs from but exceeds the raw material of its production. [207]

All representation is false. A likeness differs of necessity from what it represents. If it did not, it would be what it represents, and thus not a representation. The only truly false representation is the belief in the possibility of true representation. [208]

Property, a mere representation, installs itself in the world, falsifying the real. When the powers of the false conspire to produce the real, then hacking reality is a matter of using the real powers of the false to produce the false as the real power. This is the power of falsifying property's verification of its own false veracity, proliferating new possibilities by displacing the false necessity of the world. [209]

It is critique itself that is the problem, not the solution. Critique is a police action in representation, of service only to [210] the maintenance of the value of property through the establishment of its value. The problem is always to enter on another kind of production altogether, the production of the virtual, not the critical. The one role of critique is to critique criticism itself, and thus open the space for affirmation.

[211]   The critique of representation always maintains an artificial scarcity of "true" interpretation. Or, what is no better, it maintains an artificial scarcity of "true" interpreters, owners of the method, who are licensed by the zero sum game of critique and counter critique to peddle, if not true representations, then at least the true method for deconstructing false ones. "Theorists begin as authors and end up as authorities."* This fits perfectly with the domination of education by the vectoral class, which seeks scarcity and prestige from this branch of cultural production, a premium product for the most sensitive subjects. Critical theory becomes hypocritical theory.

[212]   What a politics of information can affirm is the virtuality of expression. The inexhaustible surplus of expression is that aspect of information upon which the class interest of hackers depends. Hacking brings into existence the multiplicity of all codes, be they natural or social, programmed or poetic, logical or analogical, anal or oral, aural or visual. But it is the act of hacking that composes, at one and the same time, the hacker and the hack. Hacking recognizes no artificial scarcity, no official licence, no credentialing police force other than that composed by the gift relation among hackers themselves.

The critique of the politics of representation is at the same [213] time the critique of representation as politics. No one is authorized to speak on behalf of constituencies as properties or on the properties of constituencies. Even this manifesto, which invokes a collective name, does so without claiming or seeking authorization, and offers for agreement only the gift of its own possibility.

Within the envelope of the state, competing forces struggle [214] to monopolize the representation of its majority. Representative politics pits one representation in opposition to another, verifying one by the critique of the other. Each struggles to claim subjects as subjects, enclosing the envelope of the subject within that of the state.

Representative politics takes place on the basis of the [215] charge of false representation. An expressive politics accepts the falseness of expression as part of the coming into being of a class as an interest. Classes come into being as classes for themselves by expressing themselves, differing from themselves, and overcoming their own expressions. A class is embodied in all its expressions, no matter how multiple.

The ruling classes maintain a space of expression for desire, [216] at the same time as forcing representation on the subaltern classes. The ruling power knows itself to be nothing but its expression and the overcoming of its expression. And thus it overcomes itself, splitting and mutating and transforming itself from a pastoralist to a capitalist to a vectoralist expression. Each expression furthers in its difference the abstraction of property that generates class as a bifurcation of differences, of possession and nonpossession. The ruling class, in each of its mutations, needs the producing classes only for the purposes of exploitation, for the extraction of the surplus. It has no need of the recognition of itself as itself. It has need only of the vector along which it mutates and pulsates. The producing classes, likewise, gain nothing from the recognition foisted on them in their struggle with their masters, which serves only to keep them in their place.

[217]   The productive classes get caught up in their own expressions as if they were representations, making the representation the test of the truth of its own existence, rather than vice versa. Or worse, the productive classes get caught up in representations that have nothing to do with class interest. They get caught up in nationalism, racism, generationalism, various bigotries. There is no representation that confers on the producing classes an identity. There is nothing around which its multiplicities can unite. There is only the abstraction of property that produces a bifurcated multiplicity, divided between owning and nonowning classes. It is the abstraction itself that must be transformed, not the representations that it foists upon its subaltern subjects as negative identity, as a lack of possession.

[218]   Even when representations serve a useful function, in identifying nonclass forms of oppression or exploitation, they still become means of oppression themselves. They become the means by which those best able to be the object of the representation refuse recognition to those less able to iden-

tify with it. The state becomes the referee of the referents, pitting claimants against each other, while the ruling classes escape representation and fulfil their desire as the plenitude of possession.

The politics of representation is always the politics of the [219] state. The state is nothing but the policing of representation's adequacy to the body of what it represents. That this politics is always only partially applied, that only some are found guilty of misrepresentation, is the injustice of any regime based in the first place on representation. A politics of expression, on the other hand, is a politics of indifference to the threat and counterthreat of exposing nonconformity between sign and referent. Benjamin: "The exclusion of violence in principle is quite explicitly demonstrable by one significant factor: there is no sanction for lying."*

Even in its most radical form, the politics of representation [220] always presupposes an ideal state that would act as guarantor of its chosen representations. It yearns for a state that would recognize this oppressed subject or that, but which is nevertheless still a desire for a state, and a state that, in the process, is not challenged as the enforcer of class interest, but is accepted as the judge of representation.

And always, what escapes effective counter in this imagi- [221] nary, enlightened state is the power of the ruling classes, which have no need for representation, which dominate through owning and controlling production, including the production of representation. What calls to be hacked is not the representations of the state, but the class rule based on an exploitative bifurcation of expression into lack and plenitude.

[222] And always, what is excluded even from this enlightened, imaginary state, would be those who refuse representation, namely, the hacker class as a class. To hack is to refuse representation, to make matters express themselves otherwise. To hack is always to produce the odd difference in the production of information. To hack is to trouble the object or the subject, by transforming in some way the very process of production by which objects and subjects come into being and recognize each other by their representations. The hack touches the unrepresentable, the real.

[223] A politics that embraces its existence as expression, as affirmative difference, is the politics that can escape the state. To refuse, or ignore, or plagiarize representation, to renounce its properties, to deny it what it claims as its due, is to begin a politics, not of the state, but of statelessness. This might be a politics that refuses the state's authority to authorize what is a valued statement and what isn't. Lautréamont: "Plagiarism is necessary. Progress implies it."* Or rather: Progress is possible, plagiarism implies it.

[224] The politics of expression outside the state is always temporary, always becoming something other. It can never claim to be true to itself. Any stateless expression may yet be captured by the authorized police of representation, assigned a value, and made subject to scarcity, and to com-

modification. This is the fate of any and every hack that comes to be valued as useful.

Even useless hacks may come, perversely enough, to be valued for the purity of their uselessness. There is nothing that can't be valued as a representation. There is nothing that can't be critiqued, and thereby valued anyway, by virtue of the attention paid to its properties. The hack is driven into history by its condition of existence—expression—that calls for the renewal of difference. [225]

Everywhere, dissatisfaction with representations is spreading. Sometimes it's a matter of sharing a few megabytes, sometimes of breaking a few shop windows. But this dissatisfaction does not always rise above a critique that puts revolt squarely in the hands of some representative or other, offering only another state as an alternative—even if only a utopian one. [226]

Violence against the state, which rarely amounts to more than throwing rocks at its police, is merely the desire for the state expressed in its masochistic form. Where some call for a state that embraces their representation, others call for a state that beats them up. Neither is a politics that escapes the desire cultivated within the subject by the educational apparatus—the state of desire that is merely desire for the state. [227]

An expressive politics has nothing to fear from the speed of the vector. Expression is an event traversing space and time, [228] and quickly finds that the vector of telesthesia affords an excellent expander and extender of the space and time within which expression can transform experience and release the virtual. Representation always lags behind the event, at least at the start, but soon produces the narratives and images with which to contain and conform the event to a mere repetition, denying to the event its singularity. It is not that "once something extra-media is exposed to the media, it turns into something else."* It is that once representation finally overtakes expression within the vector, the event, in its singularity, is over. Whatever new space and time it hacked becomes a resource for future events in the endless festival of expression.

[229] Even at its best, in its most abstract form, on its best behavior, the color blind, gender neutral, multicultural state just hands the value of representation over to objectification. Rather than recognizing or failing to recognize representations of the subject, the state validates all representations that take a commodity form. While this is progress, particularly for those formerly oppressed by the state's failure to recognize as legitimate their properties, it stops short at the recognition of expressions of subjectivity that refuse the objectification in the commodity form and seek instead to become something other than a representation that the state can recognize and the market can value.

[230] Sometimes what is demanded of the politics of representation is that it recognize a new subject. Minorities of race, gender, sexuality—all demand the right to representation. But soon enough they discover the cost. They must now be-

come agents of the state, they must police the meaning of their own representation, and police the adherence of their members to it.

But there is something else, something always hovering on the horizon of the representable. There is a politics of the unrepresentable, a politics of the presentation of the non-negotiable demand. This is politics as the refusal of representation itself, not the politics of refusing this or that representation. A politics that, while abstract, is not utopian. A politics that is atopian in its refusal of the space of representation, in its hewing toward the displacements of expression. A politics that is "therefore undetectable, not identifiable, invisible not recognizable, stealthy not public."* [231]

In its infinite and limitless demand, a politics of expression may even be the best way of extracting concessions in the class conflict, precisely through its refusal to put a name—or a price—on what revolt desires. See what goodies they will offer when those who demand do not name their demand or even name themselves, but practice politics itself as a kind of hack. In the politics of expression, a hack may deign to unmask itself, to acquiesce to representation, only long enough to strike a bargain and move on. A politics that reveals itself as anything but pure expression only long enough to keep the meaning police guessing. Lovink: "Here comes the new desire."* [232]

R E V O L T

The revolts circa 1989 are the signal events of our time. In [233] the east and in the south, the productive classes rose up against all forms of tyranny and boredom. Farmers and workers—workers in both material and immaterial trades— all formed alliances against the most oppressive and tedious forms of the state. Mixed in amongst them were hackers, hackers of all kinds, including not a few, borne of the struggle, who are hackers of politics itself.

In Beijing and Berlin, Manila and Prague, Seoul and Johan- [234] nesburg, alliances rose up that could turn the vectoral flows of information against states all too used to policing representations by cracking the heads that disputed them. The cracking of heads confronted the hacking of codes, and the hack won out.

If only for the moment. What the revolts of 1989 achieved [235] was the overthrow of regimes so impervious to the recognition of the value of the hack that they had starved not only their hackers but also their workers and farmers of any increase in the surplus. With their cronyism and kleptocracy, their bureaucracy and ideology, their police and spies, they starved even their pastoralists and capitalists of innovative transformation and growth. The revolt of 1989 put an end to all that.

[236] It did not succeed everywhere. In the four most populous states, in China, Russia, India and Indonesia, there was no successful break with the old order. India took a reactive turn toward spiritual nationalism. Russia sank in kleptocracy and control by the secret police. Indonesia saw a bold but fragile and incomplete democratic revolt. In China, the Goddess of Democracy stood briefly in Tiananmen Square, before becoming a global expression of a fugitive movement.

[237] In the "frontline states" of the old cold war, the forces of revolt were most successful. In Taiwan, Korea, Thailand and the Philippines; in Czechoslovakia, East Germany, Poland, Hungary, Slovenia and the Baltic states, the forces of revolt pushed the old ruling classes toward a new state form, in which further movements toward abstraction at least have a fighting chance.

[238] In Latin America, the so-called "transition" produced mixed results, undermining authoritarian states, but also undermining the socialized property of the productive classes through privatization and "austerity" budgets. In the Middle East, the ruling classes mostly used the state as a bulwark against an opening to the world, at the price of increased repression and underdevelopment, or corruption and theft in those states where oil clouds the waters. In Africa, democratic movements rarely made much headway against the

tidal forces of ethnic division, that poisonous legacy of colonialism, or against the new colonialism of vectoral power.
South Africa was a signal exception, and inspiration to the
world.

The revolts that group around that noisy year of 1989 [239]
achieved mixed results. But they put the state on notice everywhere that in the vectoral age, any state that cannot recognize the value of the hack, that cannot incorporate transformation into its being, will soon be forced to find more
and more extreme diversions for the desires of the productive classes.

The productive classes have seen what the world has to of- [240]
fer, and they want it all. There is no stopping them. Whatever qualms the good people of the overdeveloped world
may have about the bounty of the vector, the good life of
consumption and equivocal liberty that everyone now sees
courtesy of telesthesia, the rest of the world is coming to
get it, ready or not. "Those who are against, while escaping
from the local and particular constraints of their human
condition, must also continually attempt to construct a new
body and a new life."* And not just any body—an abstract
body, a body of expression.

The revolts of 1989 overthrew boredom and necessity . . . [241]
at least for a time. They put back on the world historical
agenda the limitless demand for free expression . . . at least
for a time. They revealed the latent destiny of world history
to express the pure virtuality of becoming . . . at least for
a time. But then new states cobbled themselves together

claiming legitimacy as representations of what revolt desired. Oh, what a time we had.

[242] The revolts of 1989 opened the portal to the virtual, but the states that regrouped around this opening soon closed it. They affirmed new theories of transformation, which were quickly rewritten as the end of history. What the revolts really achieved was the making of the world safe for vectoral power. The opening was in the end a relative, not an absolute one. The failed state-capitalism of the east and klepto-capitalism of the south may have been overthrown by a limitless desire, but that desire soon had to confront the actuality of becoming a free trade zone for an emerging global alliance of ruling classes, and a dumping ground for the consumable images of the vectoral economy.

[243] New circumstances call for new theories, and new practices, but also for the cultivation of variants, alternatives, mutant strains. The revolts of 1989 may have flourished and withered, but are a seed stock for future movements. So long as there is a past, there is a future; so long as there is memory, there is possibility. Debord: "theories are made only to die in the war of time."*

[244] The so-called anti-globalization protests from the late 90s on—Seattle, Genoa—are an offshoot of these fertile events of 1989, but an offshoot that does not know the current to which it truly belonged. This heterogeneous movement of revolt in the overdeveloped world intuits the rising vectoral power as a class enemy, but all too often it allowed itself to be captured by the partial and temporary interests of local

capitalist and pastoralist classes. It did not quite grasp how to connect its desires to those of the underdeveloped world, to which in some ways it is an impediment.

But this revolt is in its infancy. It has yet to discover the con- [245] nection between its engine of limitless desire and free expression, and the art of making tactical demands. It has yet to discover how and when, and in whose interest, to mask its faceless free expression with a representation of interests that corresponds to the broadest coalition of class forces for a free and just future. Or rather, to rediscover, as all this is already known in the secret history of revolt—that other knowledge and knowledge of the other.

There are two directions in politics, both of which can be [246] found in the class struggle within nations and the imperial struggle between nations. One direction is the politics of the envelope, or the membrane. It seeks to shelter within an imagined past. It seeks to use national borders as a new wall, a screen behind which unlikely alliances might protect their existing interests in the name of a glorious past. Deleuze: "Their method is to oppose movement."* The politics it opposes is the politics of the vector. This other politics seeks to accelerate toward an unknown future. It seeks to use international flows of information, trade or activism as the eclectic means for struggling for new sources of wealth or liberty that overcomes the limitations imposed by national or communal envelopes.

Neither of these politics corresponds to the old notion of [247] a left or right, which the revolutions of 1989 have definitively overcome. Envelope politics brings together Luddite impulses from the left with racist and reactionary impulses from the right in an unholy alliance against new sources of power. Vectoral politics rarely takes the form of an alliance, but constitutes two parallel processes locked in a dialogue of mutual suspicion, in which the liberalizing forces of the right and the social justice and human rights forces of the left both seek non-national and transnational solutions to unblocking the system of power which still accumulates at the national level.

[248] Contrary to a popular myth, the revolts of 1989 dealt a blow to the right, not the left. The collapse of Stalinism removed the external force that kept the enveloping and vectoral forces of the right together. The political forces of the right, which represent in their purest form the compromises acceptable to the ruling classes, have had to reassemble from the ruins of the cold war the elements of their alliance within which the more extreme expressions of populism, nationalism and racism can be tamed—but retained—in the service of the ruling class.

[249] The political forces of the left, which stretch wide to accommodate every interest the producing classes must embrace to achieve some grasp upon state power, has experienced no such clarifying moment. The left does not yet know that it faces a choice between the blur of vectoral internationalism and the fictive identities of nationalism. It has not yet articulated an alternative global democracy that can secure popular support. It has not yet found the formula for containing and defusing jingoistic and regional particularism. The left, when in power, zigzags anxiously between

tactical concessions to one side or the other, whittling away its broad support from both ends at once.

Globalism, as the transcendent power of the vectoralist [250] class over the world, is hardly a palatable option; but neither is conceding to the unjust demands of local and particular interest, which refuses the call of an abstract, global justice, and hunkers down behind the screen that surrounds the state. Since that screen is also the property of the vectoralist class, this is hardly an alternative, simply the same ends reached by means of the objectification of another desire. Either way, it's not much of a plan: accelerated progress into hell, or the permanent purgatory of arresting the current balance of injustice.

There is a third politics, which stands outside the alliances [251] and compromises of the post-89 world. Where both envelope and vectoral politics are representative politics, which deal with aggregate party alliances and interests, this third politics is a stateless politics, which seeks escape from politics as such. The third politics is a politics of the hack, inventing relations outside of representation. Since representations inevitably fail to live up to their promises in actuality, there's not much to lose from an opening towards politics beyond it. Rather than a representative politics, representing advocacy of movement or opposition to movement, there is an expressive politics that escapes representation. Blissett: "Do not advance the action according to a plan."*

Representative politics is a politics that struggles to secure [252] for the classes allied in struggle command of property, be it public or private. Expressive politics seeks to undermine property itself. Expressive politics is not the struggle to collectivize property, for that is still a form of property. The collectivist mode of state administered property was shown to be bankrupt by the revolutions of 1989, as was the kleptocracy of the south, where state and private ruling interests were one and the same. Expressive politics is the struggle to free what can be free from both versions of the commodity form: its totalizing market form, and bureaucratic state form.

[253] What may be free from the commodity form altogether is not land, not capital, but information. All other forms of property are exclusive. The ownership by one excludes, by definition, the ownership by another. The class relation may be mitigated, but not overcome. The vectoralist class sees in the development of vectoral means of production and distribution the ultimate means to commodify the globe through the commodification of information. But the hacker class can realize from the same historic opportunity that the means are at hand to decommodify information. Information is the gift that may be shared without diminishing anything but its scarcity. Information is that which can escape the commodity form altogether. Information escapes the commodity as history and history as commodification. It frees abstraction from its commodified phase.

[254] Talk of an end to information as property makes lawyers and liberals nervous. Lessig: "To question the scope of 'property' is not to question property."* But why not? Why just a limited critique of a few vectoral monopolists—as if

the cancer of commodification is restricted to monopoly. Perhaps, where information is concerned, the commodity form is the cancer and monopolies are merely walking dead.

Politics can become expressive only when it is a politics of [255] freeing the virtuality of information. In liberating information from its objectification as a commodity, it liberates also the subjective force of expression. Subject and object meet each other outside of their mere lack of each other, by their desire merely for each other, by desire as managed by the state in the interests of maintaining the commodity form of scarcity.

Expressive politics becomes a viable politics only at the [256] moment when a class arises which can not only conceive of freedom from property as in its class interest, but can propose to the producing classes that it is in the interests of the producing classes as a whole. That class is the hacker class, which invents the abstraction of the subject and of the object, in which both meet outside the constraint of scarcity and lack, and meet to affirm each other in new forms of expression, rather than in the sad dance of unfulfilled lack.

This expressive politics does not seek to overthrow the [257] state, or to reform its larger structures, or to preserve its structure so as to maintain an existing coalition of interests. It seeks to permeate existing states with a new state of existence. It spreads the seeds of an alternative practice of everyday life.

STATE

The state is first and last an envelope, a permeable membrane, a skin, within which wells an interiority. This interiority comes to know itself as its representation—as a unified, abstract but limited plane—distinct from what it excludes as outside. But the state's enclosure and interiority is only made possible by the vector, which provides the material means for producing the internal consistency of its abstract plane. This same vector which makes possible the envelope of the state is also the very thing that threatens to permeate it, opening holes in its enclosure that exceed the capacity of its representation as interiority to close. [258]

The vector comes first, and then the envelope; the state is vectoral before it is "disciplinary." First comes the capacity to subordinate the particulars of space to the abstraction of the vector, producing a homogenous space, bounded only by the limits of the vector. Extensive space is the precondition for intensive space, for the enclosing and monitoring of a world within, which may be classified and ordered. [259]

The overdeveloped world becomes overdeveloped through its precocious capacity to project the vector across space, designating the underdeveloped world as one of objective [260] and subjective resources for exploitation. The overdeveloped world protects itself within states that, at one and the same time, project a vector beyond, along which to draw resources, while limiting the capacity of the underdeveloped world to traffic along the same vector. The underdeveloped world acquires the envelope of the state reactively, as a protection of sorts against the vector, but depends in turn on the vector to construct its own internal abstract space. The vector is the double bind that both seals the bounds of the state and steals away through its skin.

[261] It is the state that manages, records and verifies the representation of subjects and objects, citizens and their property. At the empty heart of the state, its camera obscura, is the primary act of violence by which it establishes the separation of objects from subjects, and its own prerogative in policing the plane upon which they may meet. The vectoral state, which employs every technology for the refinement of this most abstract plane upon which objects and subjects meet, produces the most pervasive and subtle terrain of conflict and negotiation for the contending classes. The state brings classes into being as a representative politics that is also a politics of representation. All classes struggle or collude with each other directly, but their direct contact is partial and particular. It is their contact upon the plane of representation created by the state that is abstract and formal.

[262] The state is not only a machine for defining forms of property and arbitrating competing claims to property, it also transfers property through taxation and transfer. Classes

struggle over who is taxed and at what rate, and also over the transfer of tax revenue by the state to classes or class fractions. Once the productive classes succeed, even in part, in their struggle to socialize property through the state, the property owning classes seek to limit the state's redistributive powers.

The state constitutes the plane upon which classes come to [263] represent their interests as class interests, but also where classes seek to turn local and particular conflicts not of a class nature to their advantage. Through its disposition of the share of the surplus it appropriates as taxation, the state gives expression to existing interests. There may be representatives of collective regional interest, the interests of generations or genders, ethnicities or industries. The state may also create interests through its transfers of socialized property, such as pensioners, civil servants or the military. Thus the state, besides constituting the plane of abstraction for class conflict, adds to it dimensions of possible conflict and alliance by providing resources and recognition for other interests and desires. Whatever desire exceeds or falls short of commodification seeks a home in the state.

All of these other representative interests have the power [264] to limit the capacity for action of the state, or even to thwart its capacity to function. Yet it is only the interests of classes that determine the positive dynamic of state and society. Other representations may capture the state, causing the state, in turn, to capture development and retard it. Only class interests prod and push the state toward the production of a surplus and the production of history.

[265]   As a class finds an abstraction that suits its interests, that presents a plane upon which to develop and turn the general development to its advantage, it seeks through the state to represent this interest as if it were the general interest, and to use the state to head off the development of abstractions that do not enhance and affirm its power. Through its ability to police representation, the state acts as a brake on new expressions which fall outside what the state recognizes as licit relations between objects and subjects. When the state recognizes intellectual property, it creates a plane upon which the vectoral class can develop as the leading class, the one in possession of the most abstract plane upon which objects and subjects may be brought together productively. At the same time, the state takes it upon itself to police the vector, to contain information within property, to halt any hack outside the class interest of the vectoral class.

[266]   The vectoral class seeks to capture the state by depriving other classes of the free flow of information with which they may contest its representations of the collective interest. The vectoral class captures information flows within the commodity form and perverts the free flow of information. This deprives the hacker class of a considerable part of its capacity for free expression and forces it into a subordinate relation to the vectoralist interest. It also deprives other classes of their means of contesting the grip on the state of the vectoral interest, and the representation of the vectoral interest as the general interest.

[267]   The state polices the rights of subjects as well as the properties of objects. The state may be an abstract state or it may be a particular state. A particular state is one in which

some subjective representations have superior rights to others. While all states exclude some representations, and maintain their envelope through this capacity to exclude, the abstract state embraces the widest range of representations as holding equally valid claims and does not question them as to their truth-value. The particular state arises out of the exploitation of non-class antagonisms for class ends. The ruling classes exploit ethnic, religious or gender differences among the producing classes to divide and rule. This rule is purchased at the price of the suppression of some part of the productive capacity of the subordinate classes.

The abstract state will always be the most just and efficient vehicle for managing representations, but there is always something that is beyond its ken. There is always some hack that eludes or escapes its representational net. The hacker interest always points beyond a given abstraction of the state. Only after the state has accepted without question the most obvious differences of race, gender, sexuality or faith is the hacker state even conceivable, as a space for expression free from the sanction of the policing of representation. But while there may be an interest for hackers in preferring certain kinds of state to others, the state is still always a vehicle that is caught up in the violence of representation and counter representation, upon which flows of resource or liberty may hinge, but which is ultimately only in existence to help or hinder the establishment of a productive relation between classes. [268]

The vectoral class also presents itself as the advocate and defender of the abstract state. The vectoral class is all for tolerance and diversity, even affirmative action—so long as this [269] applies only to representations. To the vectoral class, all representations ought to be free to find their value as objects of commodification; all subjects ought to be free to find the representations they want to value. To the vectoral class, the abstract state is the state best able to open the whole of culture to commodification. But that is as far as it goes. The vectoral state is an abstract state, but not one that can look beyond a purely formal equality of representations toward an equal share of the surplus, let alone embrace a politics of expression beyond representation. The vectoral state encourages diversity in the content of representations as a cover while abolishing diversity in the form of representations. All information is to be subordinated to the private property form.

[270] The domination of one form of property is not conducive to the interests of the hacker class. Where the gift relation dominates, as in traditional societies, reciprocal obligation in predetermined forms renders the hack reactive and particular. It rarely reaches its fully abstract form. Where collectivized state property dominates, the hack is impeded by the direct dependence of the hacker on the bureaucratic form of capitalist and pastoralist domination. Where private property dominates, as in the vectoral world, it accelerates the hack by recognizing it as private property, but thereby channels the hack into the relentless reproduction of the commodity form.

[271] The hacker class knows that while it exceeds every representation, and expresses the virtuality of matter and information in its innovation, it is also potentially the producer

of a host of dangers. The hack may be as destructive as it is productive—but only potentially. It is not hackers who poison the waters, or enrich the plutonium, or genetically modify the crops, or inculcate the dangerous creeds, but it is hackers who hack these bright new possibilities into being. It is the ruling classes who subordinate the potential of the hack to its commodified form, who turn potential dangers into actual ones. Yet they deflect the legitimate fears of the other productive classes onto the hacker class, and confirm it with selective uses of the punitive powers of the state to contain the productive potential of the hack. The vectoral class practices this kind of statecraft as a veritable art-form, stroking popular anxiety by criminalizing some marginal forms of hacking that would assert their independence from the commodifed form.

The class interest of the working and farming classes is in [272] the production of a surplus, the wresting of freedom from necessity. The class interest of hackers is in the free and open expression of virtuality. These interests converge in a state form that is at once abstract in relation to representation, and plural in relation to forms of property. Yet this is the bare beginnings of what the combined productive classes may desire. They desire a state that is abstract enough, plural enough, virtual enough to create openings beyond scarcity and the commodity.

The state has its limits. It may be everywhere and nowhere, [273] impressed in the very pores and particles of its subjects through its management of education and culture, but still it has its limits. One limit is the violence with which it founds its claim to be sovereign over the laws of representation. Challenging this limit merely affirms the injustice at the heart of the state, without in any way escaping from it. The state is limit, interiority, envelope. Transgression merely confirms it. An expressive politics is not transgressive. It seeks to escape, not confront, the state. Those who confront the state, meeting its violence with violence, always harbor the reactive desire to become what they behold.

[274] The limit of representation itself is a limit to the state. Agamben: "In the final analysis the state can recognize any claim for identity . . . But what the state cannot tolerate in any way is that singularities form a community without claiming an identity, that human beings co-belong without a representable condition of belonging."* The class that can express its desires, rather than represent them, is the class that escapes the violence of the law. That which cannot be named, cannot be identified, cannot be charged, cannot be convicted. Abstraction without authority or authorization opens the free virtuality outside the law. For contrary to the repetitive chant of the state's witting and unwitting apologists, there is always something, and something other than violence, outside its law.

S U B J E C T

The experience of subjectivity is not universal. Just as it [275] came into being with the enveloping state and the commodity economy, the subject can pass with the overcoming of these limited and partial abstractions.

Property produces, piece by piece, the armor of subjectivity. [276] This armor is a hollow shell, separating the nothing that is the self from the nothing that is the means external to it by which it comes to believe it exists.

The subject is nothing but the ghostly residue of separa- [277] tion, opening the possibility of appropriating from the self the objective existence it labors to create, and presenting the subject with the objective world as something that it lacks. The subject comes to feel its existence only through its lack of the object, a lack never quite satisfied by any particular object.

The abstract subject develops incrementally, but develops [278] apace with the objectification of the world. The history of the production of the world as a thing is at the same time the history of the production of the subject, which is to say, the production of the self as a thing that produces itself and its world as things.

[279] The subject comes into existence as an abstract insuf-
ficiency, made more and more aware of its own lack and its
own abstraction by its immersion in telesthesia. Where the
capitalist class dangles before the productive classes the
objects of their own labor as rare and out of reach, the
vectoralist class transmits everywhere, via the vectors of
telesthesia, endless images of objects of desire. Telesthesia
replaces the object of desire with its image, an image that
can be attached to any object, willy-nilly. At one and the
same time, the vectoral transformation of desire raises the
price of desire, and threatens to devalue it completely. The
vectoral class pushes commodified desire to the point where
its very proliferation opens the possibility of its overcoming.

[280] At the dawn of the history of property's abstraction of the
world, the pastoralist class merely laid claim to the farmer's
labor, and at first got limited access even to that, not least
because farmers retained some access to property, in the
form of their immediate means of production. Under such
conditions, the farmer experiences subjectivity only as external constraint imposed by the demands of meeting the rent
and producing the necessities of life.

[281] The seeds of subjectivity as a general condition are already
present under pastoralist rule, however, in the form of the
total and limitless demand that the spiritual state of the
church makes on its victims. Theology presents the subject
to itself as what it lacks, but it presents lack as spiritual, not
material; as infinite, rather than finite. As such, the church
acted as a fetter upon the development of a productive subjectivity.

Organized religion expresses the needs of the ruling class [282] in the form of a demand upon the subject. That demand changes as class rule changes. Lack no longer appears as infinite, but finite, and the means to fill it, material, not spiritual. Or rather, the spiritual lack is to be filled by the attention to material lack. The theology of the soul becomes the theology of the commodity. The capitalist class extended its claim upon the worker beyond external observance to the worker's interiority. It brought down to earth the limitless debt of spiritual usury and forced upon the worker a subjectivity that viewed work as a debt owed at one and the same time to God and Mammon. Where once, as Marx wrote, "religion is the opium of the people," now *Opium™* is the religion of the people.*

At least outside of working hours the worker was free, and [283] many workers lost the habit of devoting free time to working off yet another, more ethereal, debt. But theology lives on, and still makes its monstrous demands, if not from the pulpit, then in the classroom. If not in theology, then at least in theory. Vaneigem: "Temporal power, which is firmly rooted in the worldly economy, has deconsecrated theology and turned it into philosophy, replacing a divine curse with an ontological one: the claim that it is inherent in man's condition to be dispossessed of his own life."*

Capital merely claims the body of the worker for the dura- [284] tion of the working day. The vectoralist class found the means to assert a claim to every aspect of being, via its power to designate any part of that being as a resource. The struggle to limit the working day, while salutary as a means of freeing the body from commodity labor, no longer frees the worker from the commodity, but merely releases the subject as producer for the even more burdensome task of being the subject as consumer.

[285] In the age of telesthesia, the vector captures the body and mind and indeed soul of the dispossessed as never before. It comes closer to dispossession perfected than any other form of property. The subject at work becomes producer of commodities, and outside of work, is set to work again recognizing the worth of what the commodity represents, as its consumer.

[286] To objectify all of space is to subjectify all of time. Property invades time as well as space, and this is where its greatest impact on the subject is to be felt. Time was once a property farmers disposed of as they pleased, provided they could meet their obligation to the pastoralist master. Then time became divided into work time and "leisure." Only the latter remained the property of the worker. But now all time belongs to property.

[287] Time itself becomes the object of temporary outbreaks of revolt, ever since the farsighted communards smashed the time clocks in the workshops. But while there are temporary halts and interruptions to time in which the subject reclaims itself as something beyond itself, the totality of property encroaches even upon revolt itself, which, like exotic religions, is offered to the subject in commodified form. What would otherwise be the history of the subject's struggle to overcome itself and revolt against scarcity, becomes instead the commodity of revolt, which affirms the subject

merely in its lack of the very revolt the commodity memori-
alizes in its collector's editions.

Scarcity is based on the notion that subjective desires are   [288]
infinite, but material goods are few. Therefore some power
is called into being that allocates scarce resources. Liberal
"theology" is usually represented as a neutral objective principle, an "invisible hand," when actually what allocates resources comes to be a class power. The notion of scarcity
subjectifies desire and objectifies the means to desire's satis-
faction. They are conceived as separate things that confront
each other as if across a metaphysical chasm. It is as if all
that is desired is an object, and all objects exist to be possessed in the name of desire.

It is the propagation of the myth of scarcity itself that cre-   [289]
ates the abstraction of objectified wants and subjective desires that can only be met in commodified form. It is only in
the theory of scarcity that desire need be thought of as having an object, and that this object need be thought of as the
commodity. True desire is desire for the virtual, not the actual. Productivity is desire, desire as becoming in the world.
The struggle to free the productive classes from the commodity is the struggle to free desire from the myth of its
lack. Deleuze: "All of this constitutes what might be called a
right to desire."*

In the overdeveloped world, some of the producing classes   [290]
capture enough of the surplus to satiate their needs, if not
their desires. Their desires become their needs. Those not
working to produce commodified life work to produce new
necessities that will call into being still new objects of com-

modification, saturated in the images of desire. And there is still more work to do: every subject is enjoined to work on itself, to educate itself in its own limitless capacity to desire limited things. And yet this great production of the subjectivity of the object and the objectivity of the subject threatens to slump again and again, as subjects weary of carrying the burdensome armor of their double location as producers and consumers of necessity. At such times the state steps in to declare boredom the enemy of all the national envelope claims to secure, and enjoins the subject to labor on itself, if not for itself, as a patriotic duty.

[291] Belief in scarcity redirects the subject's experience of its own desire from the desire for its own experience, and towards images that appear to negate the subject's powers, and taunt the subject with its limits. Desire becomes a self-inflicting wound. And so in the overdeveloped world, desire comes to desire images of suffering from the underdeveloped world that seem at once "justified," in the sense of being the product of truly monstrous abuses of power, and yet far enough away as to render the subject who views the image as helpless to respond to the suffering in the image as the subject in the image is helpless to overcome their torture. Global victimization, the feeling of the self as always "at risk," is the vectoral mode of ideology. Only it is no longer global capital, but the global vector, which at one and the same time produces the actual victim, "over there," the vicarious suffering subject, "over here"—and the vector of telesthesia that governs their (non) relation.

[292] The liberal economic theory of the scarcity of objects and the psychoanalytical theory of desire as subjective lack are

one and the same theory, and both serve the same class interest. They are means by which subjects are recruited for the production of objects and objects are presented as what desire lacks. Both distract from the production of free subjectivity, which not only frees the subject from objectified desire but frees the subject from itself as subject, into the absolute freedom of pure becoming as expression.

There are hackers of subjective desire just as there are [293] hackers of the objectified world, and just as the latter hack toward the free expressivity of nature from which all objectifications arise, so too do the former hack beyond the constraints of the subject limited to its apprehension of itself and the existing order. "No society can tolerate a position of real desire without its structures of exploitation, servitude, and hierarchy being compromised."* But what is "real desire" if not the hack—the desire to release the virtual from the actual? Desire itself calls for hacking, to release it from false representation as lack, opening its expression with the knowledge that it lacks only the absence of lack. Hack the lack that lacks the hack.

The producing classes may or may not aspire to pure be- [294] coming, but still yet come to grasp their class interest in freeing desire from the constraint of commodifed objects and subjects. The producing classes continually free themselves from particular objects of desire, and free themselves from subjectivities thrust upon them in the interests of enslaving that subjectivity to particular objects of desire. While the producing classes free themselves from particular desires, they do not always take the next step, to the abstraction of desire itself from commodification. This is where hackers of both the objective world and of subjectivity can affirm their productive relation to the producing classes.

[295] Vectoral power has to respond periodically to the demand for desire as surplus rather than lack, when it breaks out from the margins into the centre of the culture. The history of culture is alive with instances of the spontaneous hacking open of information, expressing the virtuality of desire and desire as virtuality. When in power, the pastoralist and capitalist classes respond to these outbreaks with suppression, lending glamor to their legend, creating both popular revolt and the avant gardes. When in power, the vectoralist class responds very differently. It embraces surplus desire and rapidly commodifies its image. Everywhere that desire throws off the heavy armor of lack and expresses its own joyful plenitude, it quickly finds itself captured as an image and offered back to itself as representation. Thus the strategy for any desire that would arm itself with its own self-unfolding is to create for itself a vector outside of commodification, as a first step toward accelerating the surplus of expression, rather than the scarcity of representation.

[296] The abstraction of the objective and subjective worlds into information freely circulating via the vector opens up the virtuality of desire and its potential liberation from commodification. Information is "non-rivalrous"—it knows no natural scarcity. Unlike the objectified products of land and capital, one's consumption of information need not deprive another of it. Surplus appears in its absolute form. The struggle becomes one between the hacking of the vector to

open it toward the virtual and the commodification of information as scarcity and mere representation. The possibility
of an overcoming of subjectivity rests on this infrastructural
struggle. The means of production of desire—the vectors
along which can flow an immaterial surplus of information,
is the first and last point at which the struggle to free subjectivity is to be waged. Any particular image of the subject in
revolt can be turned into the image of an object to desire,
but the vector itself is another matter. The liberation of the
vector is the one absolute prohibition of the vectoral world,
and the point at which to challenge it.

The coming into being of vectors along which information [297]
flows freely, if not universally, around the world appears to
usher in a new regime of scarcity even more total than
that of the reign of capital before it. Everywhere are signs
presented as the commodifed answer to desire; everywhere
there are subjects bamboozled into thinking of themselves
as negated by the signs they do not possess. Sometimes this
provokes a reactive hardening of the subject. This produces
a bunkering within the envelope of some tradition or other
that appears to predate the vectoral world, even if, paradoxi-
cally enough, the vectoral is now the only means by which
the traditional reproduces itself, as a representation of tradition. Sometimes this hardening and bunkering in tradition
produces a violence that strikes out, if none too clearly, at
what it takes to be the images of a vectoral power this false
tradition would resist. The vector produces its own vectoral
reaction, with the paradoxical effect of accelerating the vectoral itself. We no longer have roots, we have aerials. We no
longer have origins, we have terminals.

[298]   The vectoral class detach desire from the object, and attach it to the sign. These signs of what is to be desired proliferate, even though what they signify is scarcity itself. But popular desire is never without resources, and vectoral power can be caught napping. Popular desire quickly learns to counterfeit the sign that in the first place is a counterfeit of itself. It reappropriates itself as itself, but twice removed, coveting the false and then falsifying the coveted. All that remains is to hack a path from desire's own plenitude to the immaterial multiplicity of information.

[299]   There is a detectable air of desperation in the work of the vectoral class, a constant anxiety about the durability of a commodifed regime of desire built on a scarcity that has no necessary basis in the material world. The producing classes come again and again to the threshold of perceiving themselves as capable of the self affirmation of their desires, and to a realisation that subjectivity merely binds them to the commodity, and that scarcity is the product of class rule, not an objective fact of nature. The old mole of popular desire works steadily beneath the foundations of vectoral power, undermining it from below.

S U R P L U S

Necessity is always and everywhere just necessity. That hu-   [300]
mans fuck and eat and suffer and die is the eternal preoccu-
pation of the aphorists. That something over and above necessity emerges out of collective human endeavor produces
not just history, but the production of history as a representation. Bataille: "The history of life on earth is mainly the
effect of a wild exuberance, the dominant event is the development of luxury, the production of increasingly burdensome forms of life."*

The accumulation of a surplus, the struggle over its dispo-   [301]
sition, its investment in war or feast or history writing, or
back into the production of yet more surplus, this is the experience of history and the history of experience. The gath-
ering of a surplus implies the creation of an abstract plane
upon which to struggle over its disposition. This history is a
secret history. Each victorious ruling class in the struggle for
the distribution of the surplus represents history itself as entirely of its own authorship. But in the secret history of the
surplus, it is the hack that produces the possibility of surplus
through its abstraction, and the labor of its extraction and
accumulation that constitutes history's surplus, carried over
as a murmur, from one era to the next.

[302]   Class society in its abstract form emerges out of the accumulation of surplus, and represents a break from the dispersal of surplus in the form of luxury and the gift, and the ploughing back of the surplus into production itself. Henceforth, it will be production itself that will be in surplus, seeking always a surplus of desire to match.

[303]   Theories that attempt to grasp in the abstract the productive development of human society may take one of two forms. They may be based on the concept of scarcity, and legitimize the rule of one or other class who must take charge of scarce resources. Or they may be based on the scandal of surplus, on the conviction that the productive classes in society produce more than their immediate needs, and may consider themselves deprived of this surplus. From the point of view of the productive classes, only one of these is a theory, the other an ideology—which is to say, not conducive to the expression of its interests.

[304]   That there is an oppressive experience of scarcity in the world at large is all too real, and so too is its attenuation by the vectoralization of the world. As more and more of nature becomes a quantifiable resource for commodity production, so the producing classes in the overdeveloped and underdeveloped world alike come to perceive the power the vectoral class has brought into the world: the power to steer development here or there at will, creating sudden bursts of productive wealth, and, just as suddenly, famine, poverty, unemployment, and scarcity.

[305]   The same vectoral flows of information that chasten the productive classes with the knowledge of their own tempo-

rary grasp on a pay packet and the commodified bounty, also show again and again the immense productive resources the world possesses, and the artificial nature of this experience of scarcity. The vectors along which thread the information that knits objects and subjects together in the vast global dance of productivity are the same vectors which show the world to be nothing but the spectacle of surplus.

The same vectoral connection shows the limitless virtuality [306] of information itself, which again and again escapes the commodity form and flows as pure gift among the producing classes as an advertisement for its own bounty, only to be stuffed back into the objectified commodity form by the vectoral class and held apart from the producing classes as an artificial scarcity.

The vectoral class must maintain a surplus of subjective de- [307] sire over and above the surplus of objective things. Desire must be pushed one step ahead, lest demand slacken and the useless profusion of things appear in the naked light of its futility. It's harder than it looks. The producing classes again and again create their own expressions of desire, desire outside lack and commodification, only to find that this collective expression of desire is appropriated from them, transformed into commodities and sold back to them, as if they somehow lacked the productive energy that is their birthright.

The pastoralists are the very scions of scarcity. The cap- [308] italist class maintains its rule of scarcity with some confidence; the vectoralist class maintains scarcity only with increasingly artificial means. The vectoral class commodifies information as if it were an object of desire, under the sign of scarcity. The producing classes rightly take all commodified information to be their own collective production. We, the producers, are the source of all the images, the stories, the wild profusions of all that culture becomes. The vectoralist class wrestles all this into the commodified form, while the producing classes bootleg and pirate any and every expression of information freely. Mauss: "One likes to assert that they are the product of the collective mind as much as the individual mind. Everyone wishes them to fall into the public domain or join the general circulation of wealth as quickly as possible."*

[309] The vectoralist class enlists the efforts of hackers to produce ever-new ways and means to commodify this productivity, and so maintain a surplus of desire and the scarcity of the desired object. But short of seizing hold of a monopoly on all vectors for producing and distributing information, the vectoralist class cannot entirely limit the free productivity of the hacker class, which continues to produce yet more fuel for the free productivity of desire. New images and stories, new vectors with which to organize them, new technical means of perceiving and organizing the world, new cultural means of producing experience. In its desperate need to encourage productivity, the vectoralist class induces the very productivity that exceeds the commodity itself.

[310] Farmers and workers discover for themselves, outside the commodified flows of information, that hackers exist and are struggling to produce new abstractions on both the subjective and objective axes, which have the potential to liberate desire from the negativity of scarcity. They learn to

adopt and adapt new abstractions for themselves, rather than in the commodified form in which the vectoralist class would sell virtuality to the masses.

Farmers and workers discover, with a little help from the hacker class, that information wants to be free, that its scarcity is maintained only by the artificial means of the commodification of the vector and the policing of representation by the state. Initially, the producing classes discover the means to propagate information freely as a means to acquire what it desires. But the freeing of information, even in the margins of third nature, breaches the economy of scarcity, and the separation of subject and object maintained by the object's scarcity. The producing classes are reunited with their own free productivity, at first inadvertently, but in such a way as to plant the seeds of a desire for desire outside of scarcity itself. [311]

The vectoralist class discovers—irony of ironies!—a scarcity of scarcity. It struggles to find new "business models" for information, but ends up settling for its only reliable means of extracting a surplus from its artificial scarcity, through the formation of monopolies over every branch of its production. Stocks, flows and vectors of information are brought together in vast enterprises, with the sole purpose of extracting a surplus through the watertight commodification of all elements of the process. By denying to the producing classes any free means of reproducing their own culture, the vectoralist class hopes to extract a surplus from selling back to the producing classes their own souls. But the very strength of the vectoralist class—its capacity to [312] monopolize the vector, points to its weakness. The only lack is the lack of necessity. The only necessity is the overcoming of necessity. The only scarcity is of scarcity itself.

V E C T O R

The vector is viral. Burroughs: "The word is now a virus. [313]
The flu virus may once have been a healthy lung cell. It
is now a parasitic organism that invades and damages the
lungs. The word may once have been a healthy neural cell.
It is now a parasitic organism that invades and damages
the central nervous system."* And the means by which the
word, or the virus, moves from host to host is the vector.
The vector is the way and means by which a given pathogen
travels from one population to another. Water is a vector for
cholera, bodily fluids for HIV. By extension, a vector may be
any means by which anything moves. Vectors of transport
move objects and subjects. Vectors of communication move
information.

Telegraph, telephone, television, telecommunications: [314]
these terms name not just particular vectors, but a general
abstract capacity that they bring into the world and expand.
All are forms of telesthesia, or perception at a distance.
Starting with the telegraph, the vector of telesthesia accelerates the speed at which information moves relative to all
other things. Telesthesia produces the abstract speed by
which all other speeds are measured and monitored.

[315] The development of the vector creates the space within which the abstraction of property brings more and more of nature under the reign of the commodity. Marx: "Capital by its nature drives beyond every spatial barrier. Thus the creation of the physical conditions of exchange—the means of communication and transport—the annihilation of space by time—becomes an extraordinary necessity for it."* Only it is not capital, but the vector, that provides the material means for this annihilation of particular traditions and envelopes. Capital, as a stage of the abstraction of property, enters the world only through the material development of the vector which carries it, and all forms of property, further and further into the world.

[316] The extraordinary necessity of the vector for capital leads to the capture of capital and its interests by a new ruling class that exploits capital's dependence on the vector—the vectoralist class. The vectoralist class emerges out of capital just as capital emerged out of the pastoralist class, as a specialized interest that gravitates towards the most abstract aspect of property, and discovers the leverage that control over abstraction can bring in relation to the rest of its former class. As the vectors of telesthesia differentiate communication from the vectors of transport, information emerges as an abstraction ripe for commodification in all of its aspects—as a stock, as a flow, as a vector.

[317] Even more than the pastoralist and capitalist classes before it, the vectoralist class depends on the advances hackers produce in order to maintain their competitive advantage and

the profitability of their enterprises. Where owners of land and capital may dominate through the sheer level of investment required, the vectoral class relies on a form of property subject to constant hacks that create qualitatively new forms of production and devalue the old means of production. The vectoral class invests the surplus it appropriates into hacking to an unprecedented degree, and bases the fortunes of its enterprises on intellectual property. Its investment in hacking is hardly disinterested. Its search is for ever-new ways to vectoralize information in the form of a commodity.

Once information has become the object of a regime of property, a vectoral class emerges who extract its margin from the ownership of information. This class competes among itself for the most lucrative ways to commodify information as a resource. With the commodification of information comes its vectoralization. Extracting a surplus from information requires technologies capable of transporting information through space, but also through time. The storage of information may be as valuable as its transmission, and the archive is a vector through time just as telesthesia is a vector through space. The whole potential of space and time becomes the object of the vectoral class. [318]

The vectoral class comes into its own once it is in possession of powerful technologies for vectoralizing information. Information becomes something separate from the material conditions of its production and circulation. It is extracted from particular localities, cultures, forms, and distributed in [319] ever widening circles, under the sign of property. The abstraction of information from the world becomes, in turn, the means of abstracting the world from itself.

[320] The vectoral class may commodify information stocks or flows as well as communication vectors. A stock of information is an archive, a body of information maintained through time that has enduring value. A flow of information is the capacity to extract information of temporary value out of events and to distribute it widely and quickly. A vector is the means of achieving either the temporal distribution of a stock, or the spatial distribution of a flow of information. Vectoral power as a class power arises from the ownership and control of all three aspects.

[321] The vector not only abstracts information from the particular conditions of its production, it abstracts every other relation with which it comes into contact. The expansion of the reach of markets, states, armies, cultures, from local to national to supranational forms, is conditioned by the development of the vectors along which information travels to thread them together. The vector traverses any envelope, expanding it, exploding it, or provoking it to lick and seal itself tight.

[322] The irreversible abstraction of information comes at the point where vectors of telesthesia are hacked into being that free information from the velocity of movement of objects and subjects. Once information can move faster than people or things, it becomes the means by which people and things are to be meshed together in the interests of productive ac-

tivity in ever expanding envelopes. Once the vectors of tele-thesia, with their superior speed, seize control of vectors of movement, a third nature arises with the power to direct and shape second nature. But like any everyday experience —it seems "natural." The vector becomes natural as third nature becomes historical.

The vectors of movement abstract from the geography of [323] nature, and provide the axes along which collective human labor transforms nature into second nature. Second nature offers a new home in the world, in which freedom is wrested from necessity, but where class rule imposes yet new necessities on the producing classes. The vectors of telesthesia further abstract second nature from itself, pro-ducing a third nature in which new freedoms are wrested from necessity—and new necessities produced by class dom-ination. But as the vector brings more and more abstraction into the world, it also opens more and toward the virtual. The geography of third nature becomes a virtual geog-raphy.

Just as second nature extracts itself from nature yet de- [324] pends on it, so too does third nature extract itself from na-ture and depend on it. Third nature is not transcendence or escape from nature, but merely the release of the virtuality of nature into the world, as the production of collective hu-man labor.

With the coming of telesthesia, the communication vector [325] becomes a power over and above both nature as well as sec-ond nature. The vector intensifies the exploitation of nature, by providing an ever-present third nature, within which nature is grasped as an object, as a quantifiable resource, to be commodified and exploited by the ruling classes. The world itself becomes objectified.

[326] Each ruling class of the vectoral era appropriates the world as it finds it, and transforms it into a world ripe for appropriation by its successor, deploying ever more abstract means. The pastoralist class appropriates nature as its property, and extracts a surplus from it. The capitalist class transforms it toward a second nature, a built environment in which the resistance of nature to objectification is mitigated, if not overcome. The vectoralist class appropriates second nature as the material conditions for the reign of a third nature, in which resources both natural and social in origin may be represented as things.

[327] The vector intensifies the setting to work of the producing classes, but in the form of commodity production. Not just nature is objectified and quantified, but so too is second nature. The producing classes find themselves transformed into objects of quantification and calculation. Third nature becomes the environment within which the production of second nature accelerates and intensifies, becoming global in its apprehension of itself. Second nature, in the grip of a third nature, is at the same time the workshop within which nature itself is appropriated in an objectified form. Nature appears as the world, and the world appears as nature, precisely at the moment that an objectifying power seizes it in its totality as a resource.

Telesthesia allows the quantification of all things, their [328] comparison, and the direction of resources according to the apprehension of the world simultaneously as a field of objects that can be brought into productive relation. Nature and second nature, objectified as resources, are simultaneously available for calculation and mobilization. Space becomes subject to instantaneous command. But what is rational as a particular appropriation of the world combines with every other equally rational appropriation, in an irrational whole. Or, what amounts to the same thing: considered as a static equilibrium, the vectoral order is indeed an order, considered as a dynamic unfolding of an event, it drives logically to the exhaustion of its resources.

The vectoral class ascend to the illusion of an instantaneous [329] and global plane of calculation and control. But as the productive classes of the world come to know only too well, it is not the vectoralist class that really holds subjective power over the objective world. The vector itself usurps the commanding role, becoming the sole repository of will toward a world that can be apprehended only in its commodified form. This emerging global plane is at once totalizing and emphatically partial. A totality emerges under the sign of a mere aspect.

The vectoral class unleashes this third nature upon the [330] world, and profits from it, either directly or indirectly. It profits from the producing classes, and also from the other ruling classes, to whom it sells the vectoral capacity to grasp the world in its objectified form—the capacity of telesthesia.

Sometimes the vectoral class competes with the capitalist and pastoralist classes; sometimes it colludes and collaborates. The state-form adjusts itself accordingly. The index of the relationship of the vectoral class to state power is the transformation of the laws governing vectors, such as the airwaves and networks, and regulating patents, copyrights and trademarks. When thought itself and the air itself have been subordinated to their representation as property, the vectoral class is in charge.

[331] The becoming-vectoral of this world is the release of the productive potential of all its resources, and at the same time, the creation of a category of resource for any and every thing in it. The vectoral is not only the potential to conceive of everything as a resource, but also the potential to bring that resource into productive relation to any other resource whatsoever. The vector turns particular geographies into virtual geography, offering its specific qualities as exchangeable quantities.

[332] The reign of the vector is one in which any and every thing can be apprehended as a commodity. Everything that appears is something distinct, something of value, and which may be transformed at will into any other thing, which may be brought together with any other thing of value in the creation of a new value. The reign of the vector is the reign of value.

[333] Having set third nature in motion, the vectoral class finds itself increasingly unable to control its creation. Subjectivity resides not in the vectoral class, but in the cumulative prod-

uct of its activity, the third nature that arises out of the proliferation of the vector. This third nature comes moreover to
represent to itself its own limitations. These limitations do
not escape the attention of the productive classes, who must
daily live with them. Third nature fails to allocate natural resources in such a way that second nature could ever be sus-
tained.

There may be cold comfort for the productive classes in
this. They may not control the means by which information
is extracted from their lives and returned to them in form
of the commodity. They may not control the allocation of
resources based on the instantaneous quantification of all
things in the world, but the point may be reached where no
class does. The vectoral class produces a means of domination over the world that comes to dominate even its own ex-
ertions and extortions. [334]

The vector is a power the world over, but a power that is
not evenly distributed. Nothing in the nature of the vector
determines that it must be deployed here rather than there,
between these persons rather than those, between these cities rather than these hinterlands, these empires rather than
these peripheries. Nothing about the vector in the abstract
says what flows along it must only flow one way, from boss
to hand, from metropolis to province, from empire to col-
ony, from the overdeveloped to the underdeveloped world.
And yet this is the vectoral as we find it. This open potential
yet limited application is the very condition of the vectoral.
As a figure in geometry, a vector is a line of fixed length, but
of no fixed position. As a figure in technology, a vector is a [335]

means of movement that has fixed qualities of speed and capacity, but no predetermined application. A vector is partly determined, but also partly open. A vector is partly actual, partly virtual. All that is determined by the technology is the form in which information is objectified, not the where and the how. That vectoral development is uneven development calls for analysis that looks beyond the fetish of the technical, to the form of class power that seizes upon its virtual openness and renders it as actual inequality.

[336] The whole of life in the most overdeveloped parts of the world presents itself as a vast accumulation of vectors. It is the proliferation and intensification of the vector that constitutes the "development" of the overdeveloped world. Whether this be an advance toward the furthest regions of hell or not remains to be seen.

[337] In the underdeveloped world, the vector becomes the means by which the transformation of nature into second nature is effected. But where, in the overdeveloped world, this process at least affords the productive classes the opportunity of struggling against their local ruling classes, in the underdeveloped world the productive classes must struggle against a global and abstract third nature. The resources, natural and social, that are detected and appropriated there become the means for the further development of over-development elsewhere.

[338] Such is perhaps how it always was in the colonial dimension of vectoral development. But where once the underdeveloped world struggled directly against a forcible appro-

priation and commodification, now it struggles against an abstract and vectoral power, everywhere and nowhere. Once upon a time, the colonies were ruled by battalions of soldiers; now—by a phalanx of bankers. The underdeveloped world has little choice but to acquire vectoral power for the defence of its envelopes against the vectoral power emanating from the overdeveloped world.

The vector perfected would be the relation that holds in [339] that world which is, in every one of its aspects and moments, potentially becoming every other world. That this world has not come to pass, yet is indeed the virtual aspect of the actual world as we find it, leads to a questioning of the powers that limit this potential. Constraint is what must be accounted for, the constraint imposed by the direction of the development of the vector by its commodified form and its subordination to the rule of the vectoral class.

The hacker class seeks the liberation of the vector from the [340] reign of the commodity, but not to set it indiscriminately free. Rather, to subject it to collective and democratic development. The hacker class can release the virtuality of the vector only in principle. It is up to an alliance of all the productive classes to turn that potential to actuality. Once the productive classes have actual control over the vector, then its virtual powers can be realized as a process of collective becoming.

Under the control of the vectoral class, the vector proceeds [341] by means of objectification, and produces a corresponding subjectivity. Just as the object becomes an abstract value, so too does the subject. A vectoral subjectivity arises which is not the universal enlightened subject long dreamt of in the overdeveloped world. Vectoral subjectivity is abstract, but not universal. It acquires its specificity as the internalizing of the differentiation of values that appear on the abstract plane of the vector. This subjectivity is as partial as vectoral objectivity—the difference being that an object does not know it has been appropriated as a resource by the vector, while a subject potentially does. The subject experiences its partiality as loss or lack, which it may seek to fulfil through the very same field of values—the field of the vector—that produces the lack in the first place. Or, it may hack the vector, opening it to the production of qualities excluded from the dominant form of communication under class rule.

[342] The vectoral class struggles at every turn to maintain its subjective power over the vector, but as it continues to profit by the proliferation of the vector, some capacity over it always escapes control. In order to market and profit by the information it peddles over the vector, it must in some degree address the vast majority of the producing classes in terms of their real desires. The vectoral class finds itself always opening the vector towards the producing classes and then struggling to shut or reappropriate the very desires it has called forth. The veritable riot of representations produces inevitable riots against representation.

[343] It remains only for the producing classes, addressed as if they were productive agents of desire, to really produce themselves as and for themselves, and use the available vec-

tors for a collective becoming. This struggle for class power on the part of the producing classes is a struggle for collective becoming. It joins with the planetary struggle for survival, in which the whole of nature, in all its dimensions, must appear as a multitude of living, collective forces.

The great challenge to the hacker class is not just to create [344] the abstractions by which the vector may develop, but the forms of collective expression that may overcome the limits not just of commodification, but of objectification in general, of which commodification is just the most pernicious and one-sided development. But the hacker class cannot change the world on its own. It can offer itself out for hire to the vectoralist class for the maintenance of the reign of the commodity; or it can express itself as a gift to the producing classes, pushing abstraction beyond the bounds of the commodity form. The hacker class virtualizes, the producing classes actualize.

The interest of the hacker class in the production of pro- [345] duction, in the abstraction of the world, the expression of the virtuality of nature, can be brought into accord with the needs and interests of nature itself. But this too is only a step toward another history. A history where nature expresses itself as itself, as neither object nor subject, but as its infinite virtuality. A history in which the production of a fourth, or fifth nature, nature to infinity, affirms the nature of nature itself.

W O R L D

The uneven development of the resources of nature that [346]
the vector objectifies leads to relations of exploitation between states. Those states in which the ruling class can
quickly seize control of abstractions and productively apply
them to resources acquire a power over other states and can
force relations of unequal exchange upon them.

The most developed states are those in which the feudal [347]
patchwork of particular property forms and traditional
means of deploying resources is quickly overturned by the
more productive, abstract and vectoral forms. Local and
qualitative property forms give way to the abstraction of
private property, which pits farmers against pastoralists, and
workers against capitalists on a local, then regional, then national scale.

At each stage of its unfolding, this abstraction of space [348]
develops out of the imposition of abstract geographies of
communication vectors on the concrete and particularized
geographies of nature and second nature. The vector creates the plane upon which localities merge into regions, regions into states, states into suprastate unions. The develop-

ment of telesthesia and the bifurcation of the vector into communication and transport greatly accelerate the process.

[349] Wherever the productive hack that best releases the surplus of production can be identified, applied and is put into practice quickly, surplus accumulates, and the territorial power of the most productive localities, regions, states and supra-states grows apace. If the hack accelerates the development of the vector, the vector accelerates the hack. Each is a multiplier of the potential of the other, and of those territories within which this productivity is most developed.

[350] Wherever hacking has been most at liberty, best resourced and most rapidly adopted, a surplus is released and productivity grows. Wherever hacking has been most rapidly applied to commodification, all traditional and local fiefdoms and unproductive pockets have been liquidated, their resources thrown into larger and larger pools of resources, out of which ever more varied productive possibilities may be further generated.

[351] Wherever hacking has produced the most varied productive possibilities, power arises that subordinates territory to its demands. Localities dominate regions, regions states, states other states. Wherever these imperial powers arise, they become a power also over hacking, subordinating it to the growing demand of the ruling classes for forms of abstraction that further enhance and defend their power. Thus the liberty that gave rise to abstraction, and abstraction to power, comes back to impose new necessities on the free expression of the hacker class.

In the states where this process has developed most rapidly, [352]
to the point where these centres of power constitute an
overdeveloped bloc of states, the exploitation of underdeveloped territories by the ruling classes creates the surplus out
of which the state may compromise with the productive
classes and incorporate some of their interests—at the expense of the underdeveloped world.

The same vectors that permit an opening of abstraction [353]
into the world, allowing the ruling classes to expand into the
developing world, can become a means to erect barriers to
protect the overdeveloped world. Thus the ruling classes
seek to open the developing world to its flows of capital and
information, but it cultivates an alliance with the productive
classes within the borders of the overdeveloped world for
the maintenance of barriers against flows emanating from
the underdeveloped world. Neither the labor, nor the products of the labor of the developing world are to be allowed
free entry into the overdeveloped territories.

The abstraction of the world that the vector makes possible [354]
is arrested in a state of development that represents the interests of the ruling classes, but in which the producing
classes of the overdeveloped world have acquired a stake
through their partial democratization of the state and partial socialization of property through state ownership. "Production of wealth in the empire of signs is the reproduction
of scarcity and the cyber-policed poverty of everything outside."*

Pastoralists and farmers unite against the underdeveloped [355]
world in protecting markets for foodstuffs bounded by the

overdeveloped state. Likewise, capitalists and workers unite to protect markets against goods produced in the underdeveloped world. An "historic compromise" arises in which the vector is deployed unevenly, and abstraction stops at the state borders.

[356]   The hacker class is also partly accommodated, through the recognition of intellectual property as property, and through its partial socialization. The high rate of production of new abstractions is thus secured by accommodating the interests of the hacker class within the overdeveloped territories. This compromise is contingent and temporary. The overdeveloped world may arrest the abstraction of the vector by turning it into a means of enclosing its local and regional interests, but the overdeveloped world also incubates the rapid hack of vectoral technologies with the capacity to overcome such limits.

[357]   The productive classes of the underdeveloped world, though deprived of resources, exceed themselves in their collective ingenuity for creating opportunities out of global disadvantage. Every resistance to their demand for vectoral justice is met with ever more inventive means to circumvent inequality and exploitation. In the underdeveloped world, the hacker class as class may not be well defined, due to the inchoate state of intellectual property law. The creative practice of the hack, however, is far from underdeveloped. It is an organic part of the tactics of everyday life among the farming and working classes, to an extent sometimes lost among the productive classes of the overdeveloped world.

The compromise between the ruling and productive classes [358] in the overdeveloped world only encompasses the pastoralist and capitalist ruling interests, who are in any case limited by the partial development of the potential of the vector from conceiving of their productive universe on a global abstract plane. The rise of a vectoralist class that profits by the abstraction of information itself rapidly overcomes this prudent limiting of the territorial ambitions of the ruling class. The vectoral class aspires to rule in the underdeveloped world directly, reaching through the pores of its envelopes, into its networks, its identities—and as a consequence provokes the fiercest reactions.

While the vectoral class played a subordinate role in the de- [359] velopment of the abstract space of the commodity economy of the overdeveloped world, it assumes a leading role in extending abstraction to the world at large. Its capacity to vectoralize all of the world's resources, to put them all on the same abstract and quantifiable plane, creates the conditions for the expansion of the territorial ambitions and desires of all the ruling classes.

The commodity economy has always been a globalizing [360] force, but under the rule of capital, the global served the interests of the powerful ruling states, whereas under the rule of the vectoral, states come to serve the interests of an emerging global power. The vectoral class detaches power from its spatial fixity. It dreams of a world in which place gives way to space, where any and every locus the vector touches becomes a node in a matrix of values, yielding objects that can be freely appropriated in their productivity, freely combined with any and every other object, regardless of distance, or the particular happenstance of origin.

[361] As the vectoral class detaches itself from the envelope of the state, it shreds the historic compromises capital made with the productive classes within their borders, and carves transnational, commodified information out of national, socialized culture and education. Vectoralists come to represent their interests through suprastate organisations, within which the ruling classes of all the overdeveloped states enforce upon others the global conditions most conductive to the expansion of pastoralist, capitalist and vectoralist interests around the globe. An index of the influence of the vectoral interest in supranational politics is the priority given to international patent, copyright and trademark protection, and media and communication deregulation. The abstractness of the property upon which the vectoral class stakes its power requires the globalization of regime of law and policing to protect it.

[362] Under the leadership of the vectoral class, the ruling classes of the overdeveloped world pit themselves against the interests of the ruling classes of the underdeveloped world, and against the state envelopes within which these less powerful states sought to limit the inroads of global commodification. The vector provides all of the ruling classes of the overdeveloped world with a direct, subtle and instantaneous means of coordinating not only the objectification of all resources, but the surveillance and deterrence of the national aspirations of the underdeveloped world.

As the ruling classes of the underdeveloped world struggle [363] to maintain the protection of their state envelopes, they restrict the potential productivity of their productive classes, and cut themselves off from the accelerated production of abstraction the comes from the rapid spread of any and every potential new hack. But the only option these ruling classes are offered is to sell out to the ruling classes of the overdeveloped world, and hand over their territories to the liquidation of local practices and subordination to emerging global norms.

Desperate for the investment of the surplus appropriated [364] by the overdeveloped world's ruling classes, the states of the underdeveloped world are forced to choose between surrendering their sovereignty or reconciling themselves to a diminished rate of growth of the surplus and a relentless diminution of power relative to the overdeveloped world.

The choices facing the productive classes of the underde- [365] veloped world are even starker. When their states lose their sovereignty, they become a resource for the global production of food and goods, which everywhere seeks to extract the maximum surplus. The state loses its ability to socialize part of that surplus as a condition of access to capital and entry to the emerging global order.

The only alternative offered the productive classes is to ally [366] itself with that faction of the local capitalist and pastoralist classes that resist the erosion of national sovereignty. In this case the productive classes may strike a bargain within a state cut off from development and left behind in the global production and distribution of surplus. Some bargain. The result is often the merging of the ruling classes with the state in a bureaucratic or kleptocratic form, which, should it become weak enough, may be subverted or even attacked outright by the military wing of the military entertainment complex of the overdeveloped world. The examples of Serbia and Iraq are warning enough to other such states to become even more repressive, devoting even more of a meagre surplus to arms, lest they fall prey to the punitive powers of the overdeveloped world.

[367] The rise of a vectoral class, within first national, and then international spaces, brings with it the demand for the privatization of all information. The vectoralist class everywhere comes into conflict with its erstwhile allies to the extent that the vectoralists seek to extract as much surplus as the market will bear for all aspects of the production and circulation of information. The capitalist and pastoralist classes were formerly content to permit the state to take charge of these activities, which they regard as unproductive, and to socialize them. The vectoral class presses the state to privatize all holdings in communication, education and culture, and at the same time to secure stronger and stronger forms of intellectual property right, even when these developments are contrary to the logic of expanding the surplus as a whole.

[368] The interests of the vectoralist class also come into conflict with those of the subordinate classes who benefited from the partial socialization of information through the state.

Some of the cost to the subordinate classes within the dominant states is offset by the exploitation by the vectoralists of the developing world, where increases in the cost of information weigh particularly heavily on the struggle to wrest freedom from necessity.

Just as the producing classes in the overdeveloped world [369] struggle within the state against the privatization of information, so too they can join with interests across the class spectrum from the developing world in the global struggle against a vectoralist monopoly of information. While in many other respects the productive classes of the overdeveloped and underdeveloped world find their interests opposed to each other, here they find common ground.

The spread of information vectors creates an ever more ab- [370] stract space within which the world may appear as an array of quantifiable resources. The particular and contingent borders and local qualities give way to an abstract space of quantification. This process is not natural or inevitable and everywhere meets resistance, but this resistance is itself a product of the process of abstraction, which makes what once appeared as natural local conditions appear as something threatened by an emerging plane of abstraction. Mere resistance to the vector takes on, willy-nilly, a vectoral form. The challenge for the producing classes is not merely to react to the vector, or use it reactively, but to see beyond its actual form to its virtual form.

The spread of the vector homogenizes space and unifies [371] time, passing through the pores of the old state borders and threatening the particularities that once resided unchallenged with the state's envelope. Those local identities that come to experience themselves in the wake of the globalisation of the vector are not its antithesis, but merely a product of the vector bringing representations into contact and conflict. The "traditional" and the "local" appear as representations when they cease to exist as anything but representation.

[372] Vectoralists of the underdeveloped world learn to manage and exploit representations of their own traditional culture for global commodified consumption. No sooner have they identified and marketed the expression of their culture as a commodity than the global vectoral interests learn to duplicate this appearance of authenticity. Unlike commodities with material qualities, information as a commodity may be freely counterfeited. But where the vectoralist interests emanating from the overdeveloped world fiercely protect their "intellectual property," they freely appropriate the information of value from the underdeveloped world.

[373] The vector transforms local representations into footloose global competitors, sometimes even bringing them into violent confrontation as it breaches their seemingly natural relation to place. But the vector also opens a virtual domain for the production of qualitatively new kinds of difference. These differences too may be caught up in the war of representation, and the policing of information's domains of meaning and mattering. But the vector may also be the plane upon which a free expression of difference may affirm

and renew itself. Heterogeneity flourishes alongside the imposition of uniform global commodity forms, as a new multiplicity hacked out of the vectoral.

The politics of globalization comes to represent the conflu- [374] ence and confusion of these trends. It pits the overdeveloped world against the underdeveloped world, and calls into being temporary and opportunistic alliances across class lines within a state, or across state lines within a class. Along both axes, the vectoral class comes to dominate all others in its ability to make and break alliances at will, through its domination of the vector, the very means of exchanging the representation of identity or the expression of interest.

The productive classes are hampered in their ability to de- [375] velop alliances, even among their own kind, but particularly with the productive classes of other states of differing trajectories of development. The productive classes mostly still exist within national envelopes, having come to perceive their interests and desires to date within the limits of national identity rather than class expressions of a transversal nature.

The state machine in the overdeveloped and underdevel- [376] oped world alike is losing its ability to incorporate the interests of the productive classes in the form of a compromise with local ruling interests. The ruling classes everywhere abandon their compromises within the state, at the expense of the productive classes. This both attenuates and erodes the representation of interest in terms of nationalism. The productive classes everywhere retreat behind nationalism at the point at which it becomes incapable of securing any but the most illusory representations of desire.

[377] The puncturing of national envelopes develops unevenly. The productive classes in the overdeveloped world maintain their power to slow the free flow of food and goods from the underdeveloped world and to maintain opportunities for work that might otherwise benefit both the ruling and producing classes of the underdeveloped world. But this only hampers the ability of the productive classes of the overdeveloped world to form alliances with the productive classes of the underdeveloped world, and encourages the productive classes of the underdeveloped world to embrace their own rulers as representing their interests.

[378] Differences emerge also in the politics of developing a suprastate apparatus capable of representing interests on a regional or global scale. In the underdeveloped world, the productive classes may identify their interests with local capitalist or pastoralist interests, who struggle to use suprastate organs as a means to open up the markets of the overdeveloped world to their goods and food to the same degree as they are forced to open their territories to ruling interests from the overdeveloped world, particularly as represented via the suprastate organs that the ruling class of the overdeveloped world disproportionately control.

[379] While the overdeveloped world remains relatively closed to the objects produced in underdeveloped world, it thereby becomes a magnet for its subjects. Many members of the

productive classes of the underdeveloped world seek to migrate, legally or illegally, to the overdeveloped world. As the overdeveloped world will not take its goods, thus causing under-employment and migration, so too it refuses to embrace this migration that it has itself unleashed. Migration further strains the potential for alliances between the productive classes of the overdeveloped and underdeveloped worlds, as each sees in the other a foreigner opposed to his or her local identity.

To the extent that the underdeveloped world finds any opportunity for development in spite of all obstacles, it finds itself the object of the surplus-seeking interests of the vectoralist class. Where other ruling classes merely want to exploit the labor or resources of the developing world, and are more or less indifferent to its cultural expression and subjective life, the vectoralist class seeks to turn the productive classes all over the world into consumers of its commodified culture, education and communication. This only further hardens resistance to the abstraction of the world and the retreat to nationalism or localism as a representation of interests. [380]

But what of the hacker class as a class? Where do its interests lie in all of these globalizing developments? The interest of the hacker class lies first and foremost in the free expansion of the vectors of communication, culture and knowledge around the globe. Only through the free abstraction of the flow of information from local prejudice and contingent interests can its virtuality be fully realized. Only when free to express itself through the exploration and combination [381] of any and every kind of knowledge, anywhere and everywhere in the world can the hacker class realize its potential, for itself and for the world.

[382] There is a stark difference between the free abstraction of the flow of information and its abstraction under the rule of the commodity and in the interests of the vectoral class. The commodification of information produces nothing but a new global scarcity of information, restricting the potential for its free expression and widening inequalities that limit the free virtuality of the vector. The hacker class opposes the actual form of the vector in the name of its virtual form, not in the name of a romantic desire to return to a world safe behind state envelopes and local identities.

[383] The vectoral spread of commodified information produces both the commodification of things and the commodification of desire. This heightens awareness of a global exploitation that benefits the ruling classes of the overdeveloped world, but it does so by representing injustice only as material inequality. The producing classes of the overdeveloped and underdeveloped worlds come to measure themselves against representations of each other. One despises the other for what it has—and itself for what it lacks. One despises the other for what it wants—and itself what it has to lose.

[384] In the underdeveloped world arises envy and resentment; in the overdeveloped world, fear and bigotry. Even when the productive classes become aware of the vectoral dimension to their exploitation, they represent their interests purely in local or national terms, and become deaf to the contradic-

tions between different local interests. The struggle for an abstract expression of the interests of the global producing classes finds itself beset by thickets of local and particular interest that refuse reconciliation, but which class awareness on a global scale is not abstract and multiple enough to embrace.

The hacker class always finds its interest in the free productivity of information subordinated to the interests of the vectoral class in extracting a surplus from the hack and from furthering only those hacks that generate a surplus. But it also finds that the vectoral class recruits more and more subjects into this world in which they appear to themselves as nothing more than what they lack, thus leading the productive classes into the thicket of particular and local representations, which are more and more the product of nothing but an abstract and universalizing vector. [385]

As difficult as it may be, the hacker class can commit itself to the free alliance of productive classes everywhere, and can make its modest contribution to overcoming the local and contingent interests that pit the productive classes everywhere against themselves. This contribution may be technical or cultural, objective or subjective, but it can everywhere take the form of hacking out the virtuality that a free global abstraction would express as an alternative to the commodified subjection that both local and global domination by private property represents. [386]

Commodity production is in transition from the domination of capital as property to the domination of information as property. The theory of the transition to a world beyond [387] commodity production has yet to make this same transition. This body of theory has been through two phases, which correspond to two kinds of error. In the first phase, when theory was in the hands of the workers' movement, it fetishized the economic infrastructure of the social formation. In the second phase, when theory was in the hands of the academic radicals, it fetishized the superstructures of culture and ideology. Theory of the first kind reduces the superstructure to being a reflection of the economy; theory of the second kind awards the superstructure a relative autonomy. Neither grasps the fundamental changes in commodity production that render obsolete this understanding of the social formation or the new kinds of class struggle now emerging under the sign of the domination of information as property. Property is a concept that occupies a liminal, undecidable place between economy and culture. Our task today is to grasp the historical development of commodity production from the point of view of property, fulcrum on which not only infrastructure and superstructure hinge, but also the class struggle.

[388] Through the renewal of history, as hacker history, emerges a theory of the vector as class theory. This theory offers at one and the same time an abstraction through which the vector as a force of abstraction at work in the world can be grasped, as well as a critical awareness of the chasm between the virtual powers of the vector and its actual limitations under the reign of the vectoral class. From this emergent perspective, past attempts to change the world appear as mere interpretations. Present interpretations, even those that claim filiations to the historical tradition, appear as cap-

tives of the commodification of information under the reign of the vectoral class.

In this tiresome age, when even the air melts into airwaves, [389] where all that is profane is packaged as if it were profundity, the possibility yet emerges to hack into mere appearances and make off with them. There are other worlds and they are this one.

W R I T I N G S

ABSTRACTION

[007] Gilles Deleuze, *Negotiations* (New York: Columbia University Press, 1995), p. 145. Throughout *A Hacker Manifesto,* certain protocols of reading are applied to the various textual archives on which it draws, and which call for some explanation. It is not so much a "symptomatic" reading as a homeopathic one, turning texts against their own limitations, imposed on them by their conditions of production. For instance, there is an industry in the making, within the education business, around the name of Deleuze, from which he may have to be rescued. His is a philosophy not restricted to what is, but open to what could be. In *Negotiations,* he can be found producing concepts to open up the political and cultural terrain, and providing lines along which to escape from state, market, party and other traps of identity and representation. His tastes were aristocratic—limited to the educational culture of his place and time—and his work lends itself to the trap of purely formal elaboration of the kind desired by the Anglo-American educational market particularly. One does better to take Deleuze from behind and give him mutant offspring by immaculate conception. Which was, after all, Deleuze's own procedure. He can be turned away from his own sedentary habits.

[011] Guy Debord, *Society of the Spectacle* (Detroit: Black and Red, 1983), 164. This classic work in the crypto-Marxist tradition sets the standard for a critical thought in action. Debord's text is so designed that attempts to modify its theses inevitably moder-

ate them, and thus reveal the modifier's complicity with the "spectacular society" that Debord so (anti)spectacularly condemns. It is a work that can only be honored by a complete reimagining of its theses on a more abstract basis, a procedure Debord himself applied to Marx, and which forms the basis of the crypto-Marxist procedure.

[021] Arthur Kroker and Michael A. Weinstein, *Data Trash: The Theory of the Virtual Class* (New York: St Martin's, 1994), p. 6. The great merit of this book is to have grasped the class dimension to the rise of intellectual property. It remains only to examine intellectual property as property to arrive at what K+W leave uncharted—the class composition of the new radical forces that might oppose it. *Data Trash* identifies the new ruling class formation as the "virtual class," whereas *A Hacker Manifesto* prefers not to offer the virtual up as semantic hostage to the enemy.

CLASS

[024] Karl Marx and Friedrich Engels, "Manifesto of the Communist Party," in *The Revolutions of 1848: Political Writings,* vol. 1, ed. David Fernbach (Harmondsworth: Penguin, 1978), pp. 98, 86. Karatani would see the property question coming from Marx, but the state ownership answer as belonging to Engels, and a distortion of Marx's whole trajectory. See Kolin Karatani, *Transcritique: On Kant and Marx* (Cambridge MA: MIT Press, 2003). *A Hacker Manifesto* is clearly neither an orthodox Marxist tract nor a post-Marxist repudiation, but rather a crypto-Marxist reimagining of the materialist method for practicing theory within history. From Marx one might take the attempt to discover abstraction at work in the world, as an historical process, rather than as merely a convenient category in thought with which to create a new intellectual product. Crypto-Marxist thought might hew close to the multiplicity of the time of everyday life, which calls for a reinvention of theory in every moment, in fidelity to the moment, rather than a repetition of a representation of a past orthodoxy, or a self-serving "critique"

ment of the property form. Negri, who had so much to say about the recomposition of the working class in the overdeveloped world, and how the energies of the productive classes drive the commodity economy from below, does not quite find a new language adequate to the historical moment, when labor is pushed to the periphery and an entirely new class formation arises in the overdeveloped world.

EDUCATION

[051] Stanley Aronowitz, *The Knowledge Factory* (Boston: Beacon Press, 2000), p. 10. Critical theory that does not turn upon its own implication within the commodification of knowledge is merely hypocritical theory. In Aronowitz we find the essential data for establishing that this institutional context is not a neutral one. He might also be an exemplary figure for imagining ways of configuring a practice within education that advances the cause of knowledge.

[057] Bill Readings, *The University in Ruins* (Cambridge, Mass.: Harvard University Press, 1996), p. 191. The limit to this intriguing critique is that it discovers symptoms within education of processes going on without that it does not trace beyond the walls of the academy, into the rise of the vectoralist class. Readings imagines a free and open process of inquiry, but it is limited to the humanities and to quite specific kinds of humanities scholarship at that, thereby only reinforcing prejudices between "fields." His version of a free and open practice of knowledge is only imaginable within the homogenous, segmented and continuous time of the educational apparatus. Readings proposes a narrative in which the utopian promise of education is the best of all possible worlds for knowledge. Knowledge is betrayed only in the era of "globalization," which is when the vectoral class commodifies it under the cover of the rhetoric of "excellence." This ignores the long history of education as a regime of scarcity. Readings naturalizes education as the home of

knowledge, thus obscuring it from critique. This is ultimately a work not of critical but of hypocritical theory, unable to examine its own conditions of production.

[062] Karl Marx, "Critique of the Gotha Program," in *The First International and After: Political Writings*, vol. 3, ed. David Fernbach (Harmondsworth: Penguin Books, 1974), p. 347. With the canonization—and commodification—of Marx's major works as fit matter for the educational process, a crypto-Marxist project of renewal might best look to the texts that the educational apparatus considers marginal. Texts, for instance, that are bound to the events of their time, rather than which could be taken to unfold in something like the universal and homogenous time of the education industry. This particular text has the added joy of being a place where Marx most clearly distances himself from the "Marxists" who were already turning critique into dogma. It is the place where Marx himself is already a crypto-Marxist, differentiating his thought from any callow representation.

[069] Alexander Bard and Jan Söderqvist, *Netocracy: The New Power Elite and Life after Capitalism* (London: Reuters, 2002), p. 107. See also Slavoj Zizek, *Organs without Bodies: On Deleuze and Consequences* (New York: Routledge, 2004), pp. 192–195. In what B+S propose as an emerging "informationalist" order, the reigning ideology, or "assumed constant," is no longer God or Man but the Network. As this is a transitional time, there is turbulence, as the Humanist constant collapses and a new constant struggles to emerge. There is the deconstruction of the Humanist constant, its mere displacement as Language or the Subject, and there are desperate attempts to shore it up—what B+S call hyper-egoism, hyper-capitalism, hyper-nationalism. The decline of capitalist era social institutions is the sign for B+S of a rise of informationalism and what they term a "netocratic" ruling class. The media, released from their dependence on the state, devalue politics. Media become a separate sphere, no longer standing in a relation of representation to a bourgeois public

sphere. Information has become a new kind of religious cult. The fields of economics, infonomics, and biology are merging around the concept of information as pure quantity. Quality has been all but extinguished as a value. But information is not the same as knowledge. Information becomes a cheap and plentiful commodity, whereas what has value is exclusive knowledge, the effective overview, the timely synthesis. B+S argue that an endless proliferation of information, viewpoints, and interests might work just as well as censorship and repression in maintaining the new ruling class prerogatives. The aesthetic and political task is not to proliferate or to aggregate but to qualify—and this is the essence of netocratic power. B+S see a renegade faction of the netocratic class breaking ranks and going over to the side of the subordinate classes. Their netocratic class is an amalgam of the vectoralist and hacker interest, as they do not clearly distinguish these by asking the "property question." Like Himanen, they confuse the genuinely innovative with the merely entrepreneurial.

[070] Richard Stallman, quoted in Sam Williams, *Free as in Freedom: Richard Stallman's Crusade for Free Software* (Sebastapol, Calif.: O'Reilly, 2002), p. 76. See also Richard Stallman, *Free Software, Free Society: Selected Essays* (Boston: GNU Press, 2002). After an exemplary career hacking software, Stallman turned to hacking the politics of information. His Free Software movement challenges the notion that copyright is a natural right. And yet he does not attack the vectoralist class head on. He uses copyright law against itself, as the instrument for creating an enforceable freedom, rather than use intellectual property law as enforceable unfreedom. Stallman's General Public License insists not only that what is released under the license may be shared, but that modified versions that incorporate material issued under this license must also be free. While Stallman repeatedly states that he is not against business, he stakes out a quite different understanding of an economy of information. For Stallman, the artificial scarcity created by hoarding information in unethi-

cal. If he likes something, he wants to share it. Free software is based in the social advantage of cooperation and the ethical advantage of respecting the user's freedom. It is explicitly a step toward a post-scarcity world. He sees free software as a practical idealism that spreads freedom and cooperation—the "hacker ethic." He distinguishes Free Software from Open Source. Open Source is a development methodology; Free Software is a social movement. Stallman complements his practical efforts to spread free software under the General Public License with a critique of what has become of the copyright system. Stallman insists that in the United States copyright began not as a natural right but an artificial monopoly—originally for a limited time. Copyright provides benefits to publishers and authors not for their own sake but for the common good. It was supposed to be an incentive to writing and publishing more. However, writers must cede rights to publishers in order to get published. Writers do not own the means of production and distribution to realize the value of their works, and so they lose control over the product of their labor. As publishers accumulate wealth in the form of exploitable copyrights, the legitimation of copyright shifts from the common interest of a community of readers to a "balance" of interests between writers and readers. Or rather, between readers and publishers. Where copyright licensed temporary monopolies in the interests of the common good, the emerging regime of "intellectual property" rights protects the interests of publishers—of the vectoralist class—as an interest in and of itself. What had to be justified under copyright was the artificial monopoly; what has to be mystified under intellectual property is how it represents the "common interest." What, in any case, is being "balanced"? The reader's freedom to do whatever she or he wants with information, or the reader's interest in the production of more of it? Under the intellectual property regime, only the latter is a "right," not the former. The reader's right is merely the right to purchase intellectual property. Even if we accept the dubious assumption that intellectual property maximizes production, what it maximizes is the production of unfreedom. Having lost the right to plagiarize and co-opt and modify works as they please, readers find their only right is to purchase works from publishers. Publishers then claim that anything that takes away their sales is "piracy." Authors find themselves no better off than readers (or listeners or viewers). We confront a vectoralist class that now claims its rights are paramount. The public good is to be measured by the margins of the vectoralist industries and by nothing else. Having secured its interests thus far, the vectoralist class then argues for complete enclosure within property of every aspect of information. They want to encrypt information, binding it artificially to particular material objects. They want criminal sanctions for anyone else who breaches this now absolute private property right. Patents, as Stallman points out, function very differently from copyrights, and yet the end result is the same—the securing of information as property that has equivalent value on the abstract terrain of commodification. Unlike copyrights, patents are not automatic but have to be registered, producing a time-consuming lottery for hackers who sometimes never know who holds a patent on what. This is less of a burden for the vectoralist class. Vectoral businesses accumulate portfolios of patents and cross-license to one another, enhancing one another's quasi-monopoly position. For Stallman what is most galling about the enclosure of information within property is not so much a scarcity of innovation as a scarcity of cooperation—of the very practice of the gift that is central to the hacker ethic.

HACKING

[071] Steven Levy, *Hackers: Heroes of the Computer Revolution* (New York: Penguin, 1994), p. 23. This is the classic journalistic account of the hacker as computer engineer, and the struggles of hackers to maintain the virtual space for the hack against the forces of commodified technology and education—and the

looming behemoth of the military entertainment complex. A study of these exemplary stories quickly gives the lie to the canard that only by making information property can "incentives" be introduced that will advance the development of new concepts and new technologies. The hackers at work in Levy's book produce extraordinary work out of desires shaped almost exclusively by the gift economy. The autonomous, self-generating circuits of prestige of the gift economy produce self-generating circuits of extraordinary innovation.

[072] Pekka Himanen, *The Hacker Ethic and the Spirit of the Information Age* (New York: Random House, 2001), pp. 7, 18, 13. If *A Hacker Ethic* seeks to resurrect the spirit of Max Weber, then *A Hacker Manifesto* offers a crypto-Marxist response. Himanen's excellent work has much to say on hacker time and its antithesis to commodified time, and yet Himanen still seeks to reconcile the hacker with the vectoral class. He wilfully confuses the hacker with the "entrepreneur." The hacker produces the new; the entrepreneur merely discovers its price. In the vectoral economy, where much of what is on offer has no use value whatsoever, and exchange value is a mere speculative possibility, the entrepreneur is a heroic figure when and if he or she can invent new necessities ex nihil. Here the "invisible hand" is a poker player's bluff. The entrepreneur merely reiterates unnecessary necessity; the hacker expresses the virtual. The confusion of one with the other is an ideological sleight of hand meant to lend some glamor to the dismal necromancy of vectoral power.

[074] Brian Massumi, *Parables for the Virtual* (Durham: Duke University Press, 2002), p. 30. Never was the virtual more delicately described, nor the difficulty of opening a space for it within the vector, but outside the limit of communication. Massumi brings Deleuze's thought toward a really fruitful encounter with the space of the vector as an historical and physical space, rather than a merely philosophical and metaphysical one. But

there is still the difficulty here of following Deleuze too far in the direction of a pure, creative metaphysics, which loses the capacity to understand itself as historical, as an expression of a possibility that arrives at a given moment. There is too neat a fit between the pure ontological plane at the heart of Deleuze's thought and the "disinterested" discursive space thought carves for itself within the closed world of education.

[079] Ronald V. Bettig, *Copyrighting Culture* (Boulder: Westview, 1996), p. 25. Coming out of the critical communications studies tradition, this work covers useful ground in detailing how the emergent vectoral economy works, but which in its thinking seeks to collapse it back into the categories and experiences of the era in which capital dominated the commodity economy. Critical communications scholars are right in emphasizing the lack of autonomy culture and communication have from the commodity economy, but wrong in thinking that this commodity economy can still be described in the language of capitalism. Attention to the problem of the economy specific to communication and culture shows that what it broke free from was precisely a superseded conception of its commodity form.

[083] Andrew Ross, *Strange Weather: Culture, Science and Technology in the Age of Limits* (London: Verso, 1991), p. 11. See also Andrew Ross, *No Collar* (New York: Basic Books, 2002). If journalism is the first draft of history, cultural studies is the second draft. Or at least, so it might be at its best, and Ross might be an exemplar. Ross investigates the virtual dimension to the productivity of the productive classes. He discovers the class struggle over information across the length and breadth of the social factory. In everyday life, workers of all kinds struggle to produce meaning autonomously. The people make meaning, but not with the means of their own choosing. Cultural studies has hitherto only interpreted the interpretive powers of the productive classes; the point, however, is to make them an agent of change. Cultural studies was right in seeing phenomena in the

cultural realm as not necessarily determined by events in a given economic "base," but wrong in giving little weight to the changes in the commodity form as it expanded to encompass information. Far from discovering a realm of "relative autonomy" from the old class struggle, cultural studies discovered a realm saturated in the new class struggles around information as property, but had foresworn the very tools with which to analyze it as such.

HISTORY

[091] Gilles Deleuze and Felix Guattari, *What Is Philosophy?* (London: Verso, 1994), p. 96. Among other things, philosophy is a tool to be used to escape from the commodification of information as communication, but only when it escapes the commodification of knowledge as education as well. D+G describe in somewhat formal, general terms the space of possibility of hacker thought. But their version of escape from history can easily take on an aristocratic form, a celebration of singular works of high modernist art and artifice. These in turn are all too easily captured by the academic and cultural marketplace, as the designer goods of the over-educated. D+G all too easily become the intellectual's Dolce and Gabbana.

[104] Ellen Meiksins Wood, *The Origin of Capitalism: A Longer View* (London: Verso, 2002), p. 125. Here Wood shows how what she calls "agrarian capitalism" preceded the rise of industrial capitalism. One need not adopt all her positions in the various arguments among materialist historians to see the merit of treating commodity production historically, as having distinct phases. If it has had two phases—"agrarian" and "industrial" capital—why not a third? And why not, while we are at it, revise the terminology, from the point of view of the present conjuncture? Marxist scholarship of all kinds, in history, anthropology, sociology, political science, can be appropriated—and detoured—for a crypto-Marxist project, but this involves a very

particular homeopathic practice of reading, which completes the critique begun in the text of the world by turning the world, in turn, against the text. This is a reading which appropriates what is useful from heterogeneous discourses and synthesizes them in a writing that addresses the hacker class within the temporality of everyday life, rather than addressing the reified time and space of education.

[117] James Boyle, *Shamans, Software, and Spleens: Law and the Construction of the Information Society* (Cambridge, Mass.: Harvard University Press, 1996), p. 9. A major strength of Boyle's book is to point out the contradictions within the economic theory that this vectoralist age has inherited from the ideologues of the capitalist era, contradictions concerning the very concept of information itself. When viewed from the point of view of economic "efficiency," information should be free; when viewed from the point of view of "incentive," information should be a commodity. Boyle also usefully points out that the identification of "originality" as the governing principle of the creation of new property, and an author as the subject responsible for bringing this new object into the world, necessarily cuts out from under it the contribution of collective production of information resources to any and every hack. He clearly shows how what he calls "author talk" is actually contrary to the hacker interest. In the long run it puts information in the hands of the vectoralist class, who own the means of realizing its value. Boyle even, tentatively, raises the possibility of a class analysis of information. He does not pursue it. He does not see that the acknowledgement of the collective production of information—Lautréamont's plagiarism—is already the equivalent in the information realm of Marx's theory of surplus value. For Marx, the products of second nature are the collective product of the working class. Likewise, the products of third nature are the collective product of the hacker class. Moreover, Boyle falls short of a class analysis of the ruling class

when he mistakes the interests of individual corporations for the vectoral class interest. A Microsoft or Time Warner will try to use the laws of intellectual property to their advantage depending on the case at hand, but the lack of a consistent position does not vitiate a class interest in having access to a legal area in which rival vectoral interests spar over the particulars but are agreed over the essentials—that information belongs, as private property, in their collective hands.

INFORMATION

[130] Gilles Deleuze and Felix Guattari, *What Is Philosophy?* (London: Verso, 1990), p. 108. It is often overlooked that the departure point for this text is a critique of the great mass of punditry and mere opinion within communication. Or in other words, that it departs from a critique of the surfaces of everyday life under the rule of the vectoral class. For all its merits, however, D+G's turn to philosophy, art, and science on their own is not enough. Nor is it enough to discover the constitutive differences among these three sovereign means of hacking the virtual. The missing link is an analysis of the way art, science and philosophy are debased into mere serviceable tools for vectoral power.

[135] Michael Perelman, *Class Warfare in the Information Age* (New York: St. Martin's, 1998), p. 88. See also Michael Perelman, *Steal This Idea* (New York: Palgrave Macmillan, 2002). Nothing was more damaging to Marxist thought than the division of labor that allowed economists within the education apparatus to ignore the cultural superstructures, while cultural studies ignored developments in the economy and claimed an exclusive right to the cultural superstructures. The result was that both missed a crucial development that passed between these two mutually alienated competences—the development of information as property. Perelman does useful work in debunking the emergent ideologies of the vectoralist class, but remains somewhat fixed in thinking the commodity economy in terms of its capitalist phase only.

NATURE

[143] Friedrich Nietzsche, *Unfashionable Observations* (Stanford: Stanford University Press, 1995), p. 80. By standing outside both culture and education, Nietzsche was uniquely alive to the way both, as weak forms of power, nevertheless exerted a strong pressure in misshaping the bodies of those who practice them to their disciplines and procedures, and how they offered illusory compensations in the form of subjective identities for the inescapable fact that real power was elsewhere. Nietzsche, for all his foibles, points the hacker away from resentment and toward cunning, which is to say, away from the moral and toward the political. He is also, in the *Birth of Tragedy,* clearly the originator of critical media theory.

[150] Gilles Deleuze and Felix Guattari, *What Is Philosophy?* (London: Verso, 1990), p. 169. One of the great merits of D+G's eccentric body of work is the way it cuts across the natural / social divide at a weird diagonal, breaking open the envelopes of self and society, tracing the threads that weave these apparently autonomous and self-centering bubbles into the biological, even the geological, not to mention the technical layers. While they are not alone in proposing a decentering of the self or the subject, they are in more rarefied company in seeing the troubled and troubling boundaries of the social as also a zone to be traversed. D+G offer a line along which to think the reconnection of hacker practices in very different domains of science, art and theory that might bypass the prejudices each holds concerning the other as yet another useless layer of negative "identity."

PRODUCTION

[165] Karl Marx, *Capital,* vol. 3 (Harmondsworth: Penguin, 1993), pp. 958–959. Here is the essential tension in Marx's thought to which crypto-Marxist thinking might offer modulated refrains but does not escape. For all its violence and exploitation, the commodity economy advances toward virtuality by multiply-

ing the resources with which it might be revealed, but cannot of itself reveal it. Moreover, capitalist society is not the last word in the historical development of necessity. Vectoralist society develops out of it, and against it, abstracting the regime of property to the point where it makes a necessity of the scarcity of information. But this is the point at which necessity is no longer material necessity, based in the ontological facticity of things. It is based only on the ideological chimera that makes information appear as a mere thing. There is no such thing as "late" capitalism, only "early" vectoralism. And this is good news. The historical conditions for the "true realm of freedom" are only just beginning to appear on the horizon.

[170]   Michael Hardt and Antonio Negri, *Labor of Dionysus* (Minneapolis: University of Minnesota Press, 1994), p. 9. This is an essential point—everyday life becomes a social factory, but its reverse is no less significant. In the overdeveloped world, the "factory" becomes social. Work becomes a form of constrained play, as the vectoral class tries to find ways to trap and channel virtuality itself. It should not be forgotten, however, that in the underdeveloped world, the struggles of farmers and workers continue unabated. We are a very long way from the real subsumption of all aspects of life everywhere under the sign of the vectoral economy. But time is multiple, heterogeneous. There is no reason not to experiment with public networks, data regifting, temporary autonomous zones, strategies for tactical media—right now. Nor is there any reason to think that the leading innovations in freeing the vector from the vectoral class might not come from the underdeveloped world.

[171]   Georg Lukács, *History and Class Consciousness* (London: Merlin, 1983), p. 89. This text narrowly misses being a crypto-Marxist classic. Taken on their own, Lukács's analyses of the reification of labor are a masterpiece of discerning abstraction at work in the world, as at once a class force and an historical force. Here the text opens itself up to discovering its own moment in the ongoing abstraction of history. But then Lukács retreats, dis-

sembles, and finally—capitulates. The text still lends itself to a crypto-Marxist reading, which deciphers the lines along which the text points to abstraction as an opening, as the virtual, no matter how vigorously the author is elsewhere shoving the light it emits into the sealed file of an orthodoxy.

[172] Felix Guattari, *Chaosmosis: An Ethico-Aesthetic Paradigm* (Sydney: Power Publications, 1995), p. 21. Where Marx sees living and dead labor as an ensemble, Guattari likewise sees human and inhuman subjectivity as an ensemble. Where for Marx money, the general equivalent, makes it possible for various concrete labors to be comparable as abstract labor, Guattari points toward an abstract and machinic subjectivity made possible by the vector. Where Marx sees the object as commodity as the fetishized product of collective labor, Guattari sees the subject as individual as fetishized product of collective subjectivity. With the shift from capitalist to vectoralist commodity production, Guattari's insistence on subjectivity as a collective and productive force that extends way beyond the boundaries of the individual subject may be no less useful for demystifying the labors of the hacker class than Marx's analysis was for demystifying the labors of the working class. The hacker's residuals, no less than the worker's wages, only appear as a fair and free exchange on the open market. Look behind the individual reward for individual effort and one finds the great collective ensemble of production which is not in possession of what it produces, and receives far less than the total value of its product. This ensemble of productive forces is no less than the three productive classes—farmers, workers, hackers—at their labors, toiling away at the second nature which is their own past efforts cast in material form. With the emergence of a third nature, where information announces its break with necessity, its potential to be free of the commodity form, the possibility arises not of an overthrow but of an escape from the fetish of subject and object, and the installation of a free collective subjectivity in the world. Guattari's life-long experiment in the production of col-

lective subjectivity and of subjectivity as collective production points the way.

[175] Slavoj Zizek, *Repeating Lenin* (Zagreb: Bastard Books, 2001), p. 82. What Jerry Seinfeld's observational humor is to comedy, Zizek's observational theory is to criticism. Some of these observations are right on the money: rather than use the courts to contain Microsoft's monopoly, the monopoly itself could be socialized. His work has the great merit of avoiding problems that plague others in the post-Marxist camp. Etienne Balibar, Chantal Mouffe, Ernesto Laclau and Alain Badiou all in various ways treat the political as an autonomous realm. Zizek's "Leninism" is a question of maintaining a tension between the economic dynamism of the commodity form and political intervention. Zizek is aware of the break that information creates in the realm of scarcity, and that this has both political and economic implications. His call to "repeat" Lenin is not meant to invoke the old dogmas, but the possibility of a synthesis of a critical political economy, political organization and popular desires. See also Slavoj Zizek, *The Spectre Is Still Around!* (Zagreb: Bastard Books, 1998).

PROPERTY

[176] P. J. Proudhon, *What Is Property? An Inquiry into the Principle of Right and of Government,* http://dhm.best.vwh.net/archives/proudhon-property-is-theft.html. As Lautréamont says, Proudhon's text, which would challenge the market, ends up being the wrapping paper for goods sold there pretty soon after. Times change. With the evolution of the vector, the rise of a digital telesthesia, Proudhon's famous line could be plagiarized and reversed: theft is property. A generation raised on the internet already conceives of all information as potentially a gift, and a gift which deprives no-one in its sharing. File sharing culture has not yet moved on, from plagiarized Proudhon to plagiarizing Marx, and thinking through the more profound

challenge that the vectoralization of all information poses to
outworn notions of property as scarcity. It seems appropriate to
answer Proudhon's question by giving the url to an digital version of the text that frustrates the question. In its reproduci-
bility, the digital is always neither theft nor property, unless the
artifice of the law makes it so. The application of this line of
thought to the text at hand would certainly not trouble it's author. It's not so much a question of "steal this book," which
merely transgresses existing forms of property, as "gift this
book," which might point beyond property iself.

[195]   Matthew Fuller, *Behind the Blip: Essays in the Culture of Software*
(New York: Autonomedia, 2003). Drawing on his collaborations
with Nettime, Mongrel and I/O/D that attempt to hack contemporary digital culture in the interests of a plural and open
flow of information, Fuller presents a unique synthesis of
Debord and Deleuze (via Vilém Flusser) with creative information practices. In the realization of the potential of the hacker
class as class, the construction of new forms for the production
of information has a crucial place. Fuller's critique seeks out
objectification within the very form of the information inter-
face. Where Stallman concentrates on the production of free
software, Fuller and friends investigate the intimate vectors that
connect human to inhuman production.

[202]   Asger Jorn, *The Natural Order and Other Texts* (Aldershot:
Ashgate, 2002), p. 171. This is an artist's rather than a thinker's
book, by a sometime member of the Situationist International
alongside Debord and Vaneigem, but in Jorn's work we have a
consistent struggle to create a practice in which thought, art
and politics might be one movement, committed to the remak-
ing of the world.

REPRESENTATION

[211]   Stewart Home, *Neoism, Plagiarism and Praxis* (Edinburgh: AK
Press, 1995), p. 21. Laced with a fierce but joyful humor,

Home's provocations form a bridge between the attempts, running from Dada to Fluxus and the Situationist International, to free creation from subjective authorship and objective property, and the more contemporary concern of aesthetics to disavow originality and the formal and detached status of the artwork that stem, perhaps, from Conceptual Art.

[219] Walter Benjamin, "Critique of Violence," in *One Way Street* (London: Verso, 1997), p. 144. In this luminous, cryptic text, Benjamin—that original crypto-Marxist—locates the conditions for free community outside the realm of representation. Everywhere in Benjamin's work he is looking for the ways and means to use the information vector as a means of expression, to free it from representation. He is perhaps the first to grasp the power of reproduction to elude the "aura" of property and scarcity, and to see in the vector new tools for a poetry made by all. His vast and useless erudition has become a permanent object of fascination within education, however, and can obscure his struggle for an applied thought, in and of the vector, in and of its time.

[223] Comte de Lautréamont, *Maldoror and the Complete Works* (Boston: Exact Change Press, 1994), p. 240. In Lautréamont, all of literature is common property, and so plagiarism is not theft, but merely the application of the principle: to each according to his needs, from each according to his abilities. Lautréamont hides nothing, passes nothing off as his own, and transforms what he takes, producing the new out of the difference. Where the Surrealists loved him for his high Gothic shadows, the Situationists correctly identify his challenge to authorship as a radical breakthrough in poetry that can be generalized—poetry could be made by all.

[228] Adilkno, *Cracking the Movement* (New York: Autonomedia, 1994), p. 13. See also Adilkno, *Media Archive* (New York: Autonomedia, 1998). Adilkno, or the Association for the Advancement of Illegal Knowledge, is one of a small number of

groups who manage to discover and think through the transformation of the landscape of everyday life toward its vectoral form. In this work, they discover that the squatter's movement in Amsterdam was not just a matter of taking and holding physical space, but was also fought out in vectoral space. They will go on to think this vectoral space in its own terms, rather than as something always dependent on, and necessarily referred back to, some kind of non-vectoral social relation. They put an end to the sociology of media, so that we might begin to question the media of sociology.

[231] Kodwo Eshun, *More Brilliant Than the Sun: Adventures in Sonic Fiction* (London: Quartet Books, 1998), p. 122. Eshun's book is unique in creating for what Lester Bowie called the Great Black Music a politics of non-identity open to the future, rather than a politics of identity bound to tradition. Eshun reimagines music as memory of the virtual itself, by cutting a singular path through techno, hip hop, dub and what he calls "jazz fission." He mentions only in passing, apropos the conditions of possibility for dub, that it achieves its multiplicities of collective hacking precisely because it explores vectors of telesthesia with complete indifference to the laws of copyright. This observation could be extended to his whole study, and even beyond music to other vectors along which the virtual might flow and the hack might cut into it. The open productivity Eshun finds in the outlaw margins outside the vectoralist ownership of music remains marginal precisely because of the stranglehold of property on information. Nevertheless, the particles of the virtual Eshun finds in the pores of the *ancien régime* of intellectual property, resonate as samples of a world to come. Eshun knows this atopian realm is outside of identities of the subject, but does not quite grasp the other condition, that of being outside identities of the object as property represents it.

[232] Geert Lovink, *Dark Fiber: Tracking Critical Internet Culture* (Cambridge, Mass.: MIT Press, 2002). See also Geert Lovink, *Uncanny*

Networks (Cambridge, Mass.: MIT Press, 2002). More than anyone, Lovink (a former member of Adilkno) has shed the useless
baggage of leftist cultural critique while constantly reinventing
a practice of free media than can develop its own critical edge.
His practices of collaborative work in emergent media are a signal example of what a hacker politics might be that can work in
a heterogeneous space between the technical hack, the cultural
hack, the political hack, and which can combine the abundant
hardware resources of the overdeveloped world with the more
astute and reflective practices of the underdeveloped world.
Lovink practices a kind of "tactical theory," which abandons
the big picture for concepts that function locally and tempo-
rally. His anarchist instincts blend with a joyous philosophical
pragmatism in treating the crypto-Marxist tradition with humor and irreverence. There may, however, be a limit to how effective this tactic may be in aggregating the dispersed expressions of the "new desire" that the hacker class can identify on
the horizon and articulate for their moment in history.

REVOLT

[240] Michael Hardt and Antonio Negri, *Empire* (Cambridge, Mass.:
Harvard University Press, 2000), p. 214. Hardt and Negri's *Empire* takes a strange turn early on, when it discusses the legal
framework of an emerging international order. On one level,
this is a standard Marxist analytic technique: Look to the trans-
formations of the visible superstructures for underlying infrastructural changes otherwise hard to detect. But what is curious
is the particular legal infrastructure chosen for attention. Had
they chosen to look at the development of intellectual property
law, H+N might have come closer to a revival of class analysis.
By choosing instead international law and sovereignty, they pursue another important but not necessarily dominant dynamic at
work in the world. Following the anti-imperialist rather than
anti-capitalist strand in critical thought, they foreground the
struggle between the vector and the envelope. This is an histori-

cal conflict, partially captured in D+G's concepts of deterrito-
rialization and reterritorialization. It is by making a fetish of the
politics of vector and enclosure, and ignoring innovations in
class formation and class analysis that one ends up with a sterile
opposition between "neo-liberalism" and "anti-globalization."
In H+N, what is innovative is that they in effect shift the axis of
conflict toward two competing forms of vectoralization—Empire versus the multitude. However, since the former is in some
ways considered a form of autonomous "self envelopment," it
doesn't escape the flirtation with romantic discourses of people
and place that dogs the anti-globalization movement.

[243] Guy Debord, *Complete Cinematic Works* (Oakland: AK Press,
2003), p. 150. One of the virtues of Debord's writings is its deli-
cate, even melancholy awareness of the sea swell of time, and
how the lived experience of time sets the agenda for critical
thought and action, not the other way around. In order to resist
the authoritarian temptation to seize the moment, as if it were
an object, any political movement must know how to bide its
time. Debord's subtle approach to time is nowhere better expressed than in his film works, which lay out the whole archive
of cinema as a landscape where history itself lies waiting in the
flickering shadows as the virtuality of the image.

[246] Gilles Deleuze, *Negotiations* (New York: Columbia University
Press, 1995), p. 127. Deleuze supported, for instance, the free radio movement, which revealed all too well the ambiguities of
a politics that favors the vectoral, which furthers movement.
Free radio might have started as something cultural, as a form
of "resistance," but was quickly colonized by the forces of
commodification.

[251] Luther Blissett, *Q* (London: Heinemann, 2003), p. 635. This
remarkable historical allegory, a "popular" fiction in the best
sense of the word, is a Brechtian learning-text for an emergent
hacker sensibility. The book's protagonist, who goes by many
names and identities, discovers through struggling within and
against it how the vector creates possibilities, both for reinforc-

ing the grip of necessity and blowing it wide open. Luther
Blissett is itself a name of many, a collective pseudonym, ad-
vanced as a tactic for overcoming the grip of property that sus-
tains the aura of authorship.

[254]   Lawrence Lessig, *The Future of Ideas* (New York: Random
House, 2001), p. 6. Information is a strange thing to make the
basis of property. It is as Lessig notes a non-rivalrous resource.
Most arguments about intellectual property pitch advocates of
private property against advocates of state regulation. But, argues Lessig, before thinking market or state, think controlled or
free. For Lessig, free resources have always been crucial to innovation and creativity. Lessig offers a useful distinction between
three layers of the vector. He identifies the tension between the
physical layer and the content layer. But he pays close attention
to what he calls the "code" layer—the software that in this digital world links the content to its material substrate. The story
of the internet is a rare story in which monopoly control over
all of the layers broke down—for a while. The genius of the
internet is that the code layer allows any kind of content to
swirl across its physical layer. It enables all kinds of devices to
be built at either end. Free information is crucial to creating
new information. It's as true of computer code as of songs and
stories. But it takes more than information. You need access.
You need a vector. You need a physical communication system
that isn't choked off by monopoly control. And you need to
know the code. Although Lessig doesn't go there, one can think
of melody and harmony, grammar and vocabulary, shots and
edits as code. Musicians, writers, filmmakers are hackers of
code too. The difference is that nobody has used intellectual
property laws to rope off the English language or the 12-bar
blues as their corporate rainmaker—yet. But this is what is
happening to computer code. A straightjacket of property law
keeps it chained to the interests of monopoly. Lessig favors a
"thin" intellectual property regime. Lessig questions the scope

of "property" but does not ask the property question. He does not hack the law itself. Lessig is the most impressive of those authors who believe in intellectual policy law and policy as more or less neutral arbiters that might arrive at settings in the interests of people as a whole. But law and policy are themselves clearly being coopted by vectoralist interests, making a mockery of the constructive goodwill on offer in Lessig's work.

STATE

[274] Giorgio Agamben, *Means without End: Notes on Politics* (Minneapolis: University of Minnesota Press, 2000), p. 87. See also Giorgio Agamben, *Homo Sacer* (Stanford: Stanford University Press, 1998). Marxist thought in its post-Althusserian guise was unable to think through the becoming-image of the commodity, in which exchange value eclipses use value, opening the Debordian spectacle toward Jean Baudrillard's world of pure sign value. The spectacle may be the alienation of language itself, the expropriation of the logos, of the possibility of a common good, but Agamben rightly perceives a way out. What we encounter in the spectacle is our linguistic nature inverted. It is an alienated language in which language itself is—or can be— revealed. The spectacle may be the uprooting of all peoples from their dwelling in language, the severing of the foundations of all state forms, but this very alienation of language returns it as something that can be experienced as such, "bringing language itself to language"—a third nature. Agamben finds the emerging crisis of the state in this complete alienation of language. The state now exists in a permanent state of emergency, where the secret police are its last functioning agency. The state can recognize any identity, so proposing new identities to it is not to challenge it. New identities may push the state toward a further abstraction, but they merely recognize in the state a grounding the state really doesn't possess as final authority on the kinds of citizenship that might belong within it. The

coming struggle is not to control the state but to exceed and escape it into the unrepresentable. For Agamben, Tiananmen is the first outbreak of this movement to create a common life outside of representation. What never occurs to Agamben is to inquire into the historical—rather than philological—conditions of existence of this most radical challenge to the state. Agamben reduces everything to power and the body. Like the Althusserians, he too has dispensed with the problem of relating together the complex of historical forces. In moving so quickly from the commodity form to the state form, the question of the historical process of the production of the abstraction and the abstraction of production disappears, and with it the development of class struggle. It may well be that the coming community is one in which everything may be repeated as is, without its identity—but what are the conditions of possibility for such a moment to arrive the first time? That condition is the development of the relations of telesthesia, webbed together as a third nature, which present as their negative aspect the society of the spectacle, but present as its potential the generalized abstraction of information, the condition under which the identity of the object with itself need not reign. The first citizens of Agamben's community, having neither origins nor destinies—without need of a state—can only be the hacker class, who hack through, and dispense with, all properties of the object and subject. The gesture that is neither use value nor exchange value, a pure praxis, pure play, the beyond of the commodity form, can only be the hacking of the hacker class as a class, calling into being its true conditions of existence, which are simultaneously the conditions of its disappearance as such.

SUBJECT

[282] Karl Marx, "Critique of Hegel's Philosophy of Right," in *Early Writings* (Harmondsworth: Penguin, 1975), p. 244. This is the significant mutation in the field of ideology: rather than being

something outside of the cult of the sacred, the market becomes the only thing that is sacred. It is of course a figure that
abounds in hypocritical subtleties. Contrary to popular belief,
the ruling classes do not really believe in the market. They do
not even accept it as necessity. They use the power of the state
to prevent the free market from operating when it is contrary
to their interests, and use the power of the state to enforce it
against rival factions within the ruling classes when it is in their
interests. The task for hacker thought is not to get caught up in
supporting or denouncing liberal ideology, which after all is
only ideology, but to examine its highly selective application in
actuality.

[283] Raoul Vaneigem, *The Movement of the Free Spirit* (New York:
Zone Books, 1998), p. 37. Vaneigem, that cranky co-philoso-
pher of the Situationist International, brings the hacker spirit to
bear here in freeing thought from its implication in the institutions of education that would make it a tool in the hands of
class power. Just as Deleuze sought out a counter tradition
within philosophy, one that did not set thought up as the imaginary administrator of an abstract state to come, Vaneigem
sought out a counter tradition to that counter tradition, closer
to everyday life. In *The Movement of the Free Spirit* he proposes a
secret history for the struggle for the virtual, which a hacker
history might take, with some modifications, as its own.

[289] Gilles Deleuze and Claire Parnet, *Dialogues* (New York: Columbia University Press, 1987), p. 147. The liberation of desire, not
just from the objective, from mere things, but also from the
subjective, from identity, forms a key part of the hacker project,
precisely because it opens toward the virtual. Here Deleuze,
Guattari and the odd philosophical ancestors they assemble—
Lucretius, Spinoza, Hume, Nietzsche, Bergson—can be of use,
provided one resists the pull of the flight out of history that
happens in the Deleuze industry once the desire that animates
it is that of the educational apparatus.

[293] Gilles Deleuze and Felix Guattari, *Anti-Oedipus: Capitalism and Schizophrenia* (London: Athlone Press, 1984), p. 116. This exemplary crypto-Marxist work attempts to invent and apply tools of analysis across the economic, political and cultural realm by identifying planes of abstraction and the vectors of movement. It is a work very much of its time, crawling out of the ashes of May 68, and pointing toward the various errors that would infest radical thought from the 70s onwards.

SURPLUS

[300] Georges Bataille, *The Accursed Share*, vol. 1 (New York: Zone Books, 1988), p. 33. Bataille is an exemplary crypto-Marxist author, who in this work does more than anyone to undermine the iron grip of necessity on history. Where the dismal science of economics concerns itself merely with maximizing the size of the surplus, Bataille inquires into what can actually be done with it—other than reinvesting it in production—to make yet more surplus.

[308] Marcel Mauss, *The Gift* (New York: Norton, 1990), p. 67. This is a text that calls for a re-examination, in the light of the abstract form the gift may take in the vectoral era. Mauss's socialism may yet find its medium. Telesthesia opens up new possibilities not just for the commodity economy, but for the gift as well. It makes possible the abstract gift, in which the giver and receiver do not directly confront one another. It makes possible the information gift, which enriches the recipient but does not deprive the giver. Various peer-to-peer networks spring up spontaneously as soon as the information vector makes it possible, and call down upon themselves the full technical, legal and political wrath of the vectoral class and its agents.

VECTOR

[313] William S. Burroughs, *The Ticket That Exploded* (New York: Grove Press, 1962), pp. 49–50. Along the line that extends from

the lone beacon that is Lautréamont to Dada, the Surrealists, Fluxus, the Situationists, Art & Language, to contemporary groups such as Critical Art Ensemble, one can include also that aspect of the Beats—Burroughs, Alexander Trocchi, Brion Gysin—that experiments with forms of collective creation that might exist outside of property. Indeed what might form the basis of a kind of counter-canonic succession, from Lautréamont to Kathy Acker, Luther Blissett, and Stewart Home, a literature for the hacker class, would be precisely the attempt to invent, outside of the property form and vectoral form of its time, a free yet not merely random productivity.

[315] Karl Marx, *Grundrisse* (London: Penguin, 1993), p. 524. The material means by which the exchange relation is extended across the surface of the world is the vector of telethesia. The vector is at once material and yet also abstract. It has no necessary spatial coordinates. It is an abstract form of relationality that can occupy any coordinates whatsoever. While Marx discovers, in the margins of the *Grundrisse*, the significance of communication, he does not integrate it into the heart of his theory. When he speaks of the general equivalent, for example, when he holds up coats and cotton, and explains that it is the general equivalent, money, that creates their abstract relation, he does ask where exactly this abstract relation finds its material form, which is precisely, the vector.

WORLD

[354] Konrad Becker, *Tactical Reality Dictionary* (Vienna: Edition Selene, 2002), p. 130. Becker's text works by turning the language of communications research against itself. He turns up the volume of its pseudo-scientific rhetoric so one can hear the static of power. This text does not pretend to "speak truth to power." It dispenses with the ideology of debunking ideology. The struggle in Becker's terms is rather one of discovering who or what controls the mechanisms of defining truth and illusion.

Becker follows closely the post-enlightenment turn in the corporate rhetorics of the vectoral class, which may promote "democracy," "freedom," "rebellion" and "diversity" as official ideology, but is mainly in the business of maintaining a proprietary control over their semantic range.